*How to Become
Financially Independent
Before You're 35*

HOW TO BECOME
Financially Independent
BEFORE YOU'RE 35

JEFFREY A. STERN

LITTLE, BROWN AND COMPANY — BOSTON, TORONTO

FIRST EDITION

Library of Congress Cataloging-in-Publication Data
Stern, Jeffrey A.
  How to become financially independent before you're 35.
  1. Finance, Personal. I. Title.
HG179.S835 1986   332.024   85–23400
ISBN 0–316–81290–0 (pbk.)

HC

Designed by Patricia Girvin Dunbar

*Published simultaneously in Canada
by Little, Brown & Company (Canada) Limited*

PRINTED IN THE UNITED STATES OF AMERICA

To Mom, Dad, and Greg

Contents

Preface

When I was twenty years old, I thought that if I could earn $25,000 a year, life would be great. But when I started earning $25,000 a year, I found I was as broke as when I had nothing. And when I reached $35,000 a year, things weren't much better. Clearly I was doing something wrong. I had a decent salary, but I couldn't figure out how to turn it into capital that could be invested. I had tried to save some money out of my salary and found that I couldn't do it. I couldn't cut back on my spending and still live the lifestyle I wanted.

I had tried to wheel and deal on the side and make some money, with painfully mixed results. A business I'd created in college produced a profit. We conducted market research on college students for clients ranging from a local Chinese restaurant to Polaroid. But then I started a magazine — and lost all my accumulated capital and wound up more than $10,000 in debt.

I also invested in the stock market. I went in and out of several different stocks and bought two or three stock options. Although I made some good choices, my timing was off. I made $3,000 on the stocks and lost $2,000 on the options.

By this time I was earning enough salary so that financial professionals such as stockbrokers, insurance salesmen, and "personal financial planners" wanted to peddle their services to me. I talked to a few, but I found they offered nothing helpful. Moreover, I realized that no one I knew had made any real money listening to their advice. I could only make a real profit working with these guys if I had a sizable amount of cash to start with, but to get that much cash I would probably have to get extremely lucky with a stock option. Then I might convert $600 into $30,000. But both high-powered Wall Street professionals and experienced option investors told me that the chance of a nonprofessional getting lucky with an option was about as great as his chance of making a killing at the craps tables in Atlantic City.

I was a bit bewildered. Obviously some people were doing much better than I was — and many of them didn't seem any smarter than I. Were they just luckier?

I decided to do some research and find out how other young business people in my position were dealing with their finances. I suddenly realized that these people weren't lucky at all. The successful people I met had all handled their resources in roughly the same way.

Typically they started by carefully seeking a bargain on real estate in a neighborhood they knew well. Often they found ways to buy real estate when they had little or no cash. And even when they didn't buy real estate, they always invested in something they knew well — often in small businesses that served people like themselves and used skills they already possessed.

In order to minimize the cash required, they often invested together with several like-minded partners. They usually built a foundation with real estate, *then* established other businesses or invested in friends' businesses. (People who started other businesses before they bought any real estate told me that investing in real estate first was much easier and less risky. They noted that almost anybody can usually find a bargain in real estate with a little bit of work. And when you own real estate you could sell at a profit, a bank will be happier to lend money to you and you'll have something you can cash in if a business fails.)

Some of these people also invested in the stock market or bought an occasional stock option, but generally they treated such investments as minor hobbies. They were looking for investments where they had an inside track — where they knew something that nobody else knew about.

They ignored most personal-finance books. Most of them had read a real estate book or two after they had already started investing, but they had no use for books that simply told about Individual Retirement Accounts and such, and they didn't really like the approaches of books with titles like *How to Make a Million*

Dollars by Investing in Real Estate. None had been inspired to invest simply through advice from books. They handled their money intelligently either because friends or family members had taught them how, or because they had done the same kind of research that I was doing.

Yet every single person I met who had followed these strategies — investing in what they knew well, building a financial foundation in real estate, forming partnerships to tap other people's knowledge, skills, and capital, and later expanding to other creative, useful businesses — had succeeded in making himself financially comfortable.

Some people became well-off after as little as a year and a half of effort. For others it took as long as four or five years. On average, people who started to handle their finances intelligently seemed to achieve a dramatic increase in financial freedom within two or three years.

I didn't admire everyone I met who seemed to be making money. A few people got rich but could never be happy. They were always complaining about lack of funds even though their investments had already made them millionaires. Moreover, some people certainly did make money by neglecting ethics. It's easy to make $100,000 by finding a building where tenants can't afford to pay market rents and are thus paying far less than the market will bear. You simply buy the building, announce the rents are doubling, and hire an obnoxious lawyer to get the tenants out when they don't pay.

But I met plenty of admirable people who enjoyed the relative freedom their financial success gave them and made their money exclusively by finding and creating real value that benefited others. They didn't talk much about money, and they didn't have to worry much about it. They arranged their deals so they could treat their tenants or other customers well.

But even people who felt they'd done more than they should have for their tenants made good profits. There are enough opportunities for profit that you can treat people well and still do well yourself.

All kinds of people were doing more worthwhile things with their lives because they were handling money intelligently. The financially comfortable people I met included liberals as well as conservatives; they included lawyers, schoolteachers, bureaucrats, clergymen, and artists. Most were improving the housing where they and others lived. In addition, good financial management enabled several to support a family while teaching. Others created magazines, built a computer software house, started a consulting business, or simply spent more time with their kids. Often, possessing some nonfinancial goal seemed to spur people to handle their finances intelligently.

Everyone who was doing well seemed to be following basically similar strategies. Yet *no book on personal finance told me how to do what they were doing.* I found that most such books merely urge you to save your money, perhaps using some tax-sheltering devices. They might also suggest that you consider putting money in mutual funds or stocks and bonds, and buying a house. But mostly they just note that with diligent saving and compound interest you'll have a nice pile of money by the time you retire.

Who wants to wait that long?

I'm twenty-seven. I'm not interested in simply accumulating enormous amounts of assets. I want to manage my whole life so I can enjoy it and do something worthwhile with it. Many other people, I found, were doing that already, yet no one had really explained in print how it could be done.

So I decided to write this book. When I started, I still had only a few dollars in my bank account. I had been employing the strategies I had learned for less than a year. But I'd seen them work for enough other people that I was convinced they would work for me and for others.

In the ten months since I started writing, my own financial situation has improved enormously. I invested a few thousand dollars with a friend who started a calendar publishing business. Since I knew something about publishing, I thought it might work. It returned more than twice my investment. The coop I bought in late 1983 more than doubled in value in fifteen months. I invested some of the profits from the coop sale in another friend's company that is now selling a two-record set of television theme songs, and that business is doing extremely well.

So I know that the strategies I found other people using do work. Throughout this book I'll try to tell you the details of how to make them work.

I don't know how long it will take for you to get your finances in order and acquire the freedom to live as you want. (Occasionally real estate markets get overinflated, and you must proceed very cautiously until you find an opportunity that's a true bargain.) I do know, however, both from extensive research and more recently from personal experience, that these strategies *will,* over a reasonably short period of time, enable you to do what you want with your life. And that's the only correct test I can imagine for the quality of the advice in a book on personal finance.

Acknowledgments

This book has been a pleasure to write and research in large part because the people I have worked with have been generous with their time and advice.

I am grateful to Steve Gottlieb for letting me chronicle his TeeVee Toons business as it was going through its initial start-up challenges. I congratulate him on his ability to turn the company into a tremendous success. Chris Whittle gave me insight into investing in a small business by patiently tracing the early years of the 13–30 Corporation and sharing his philosophy as an entrepreneur.

Bill Haney, Gene Murrow, Steve Belkin, Rick Pallack, and Bruce Rueppel all went out of their way to help me understand how to succeed with a new venture. Andy Gaspar contributed another valuable perspective as a venture capitalist.

New York accountant Paul Fish spent a lot of time explaining the tax implications of all the investments to me. His work on chapter 10 was invaluable.

Jeffrey Drummond, in addition to being an excellent attorney, is adept at making corporate structures comprehensible to non-attorneys.

My understanding of real estate was enhanced tremendously by Steve Furnary and Paul Cody. I am very appreciative of their time.

Helen Rees did a terrific job of seeing the project through all phases. And Chris Coffin has been a fine editor to work with.

This book could not have been written without Robert Wood. His commitment and many talents show throughout the manuscript.

My special thanks to Dan Paisner, Joe Krzys, and Ann Sleeper.

*How to Become
Financially Independent
Before You're 35*

Building the Life You Really Want

A lot of smart young people handle money as though they wanted to get rid of it — as quickly as possible. Or as though they wanted to avoid having any in the first place. You don't have to be a genius or coldhearted or even greedy to build some wealth. Any intelligent person can do it in a few years with a tiny bit of realism and discipline. No matter what you want to do with your life — from writing the great American novel to retiring at age thirty-five as a beach bum — handling money productively will help.

Most of my friends are in their twenties and early thirties. They have got good jobs and rising salaries. But they (and I, until very recently) have hardly any capital or investment know-how. Because we have credit cards, we get a lot of junk mail from banks and other financial-service companies, but they offer advice that is totally inappropriate to our needs. We simply aren't rich enough to make big companies develop and promote investment products that would benefit us. Many of my friends don't even know their net worth or their tax bracket. If they lost their jobs tomorrow or if the freelance work they do dried up, they'd have nothing to turn to but the want ads.

On the other hand, I know a few people who handle their finances really well.

One couple, for example, has built a net worth of some $700,000 simply by judiciously buying and fixing up five old houses (including two that they lived in) and one eighteen-unit apartment complex in the Boston area. They've devoted only a few weekends a year to their investments. The husband, whom I'll call Harry, earns

$28,000 a year designing housing in a government program. Since they've owned the apartment building, the wife, Betty, has worked about eight hours a week managing it, in addition to caring for their six- and four-year-old children. Harry, who majored in math in college and also took some engineering courses, could earn a larger salary in a high-powered consulting firm, but he prefers a relaxed, easy life, and he planned his strategy to provide it. Harry and Betty, now in their late thirties, live in a house on the Atlantic Ocean that they bought for $11,000, spent $50,000 remodeling, and could sell today for more than $200,000.

Bruce Rueppel is twenty-six. He began intelligent investing as an undergraduate at the University of California, Berkeley, after a summer job in the Texas oil fields enabled him to accumulate $5,000. He put $8,700 down — part of which his parents lent him rather than paying college room and board — and bought an aging, $62,500 house in Albany, California, on a bus route to the Berkeley campus. Today the house is worth $130,000 and his entire real estate portfolio is worth $500,000.

Real estate isn't the only answer. Many people want to build something more dramatic than an improved house. And many find opportunities for greater profits — though with far greater risk — in small businesses, either their own or their friends'.

Take Maynard Tipps, for instance. When he was in college at the University of Tennessee at Knoxville, he noticed that several of his fellow students had the makings of shrewd businessmen. Fraternity brother Chris Whittle, together with some other current and former University of Tennessee students, had set up a magazine called *Knoxville in a Nutshell,* and it was making money. The year after Tipps graduated, the *Knoxville in a Nutshell* partners were working to expand to other college campuses. Tipps visited Knoxville on his way home from Army Reserve training, and they asked him to invest.

Tipps put in $4,000 (largely saved up from summer jobs in a drive-in restaurant, a hardware store, and a bank). "I was betting on the people," Tipps drawls. "I knew what they had accomplished in school, and I thought they could do the same thing elsewhere." The bankers in his family didn't like the idea. "They thought I should keep all my money in a rainy-day fund," says Tipps. " 'You're just taking a flyer on something,' they said."

The business, which was called 13–30 Corp. because the partners believed they knew how to communicate with people between the ages of thirteen and thirty, made progress. *Nutshell* magazine was widely distributed at large universities across the country. Advertisers were buying space, but because of the costs of expansion, more money still went out than came in. As Tipps began his career as a lawyer, he continued to invest in 13–30, ultimately putting in $23,000.

It took five years before the 13–30 Corp. produced a positive cash flow. Seven years after the business started, a giant Swedish publisher bought half the company's stock, bringing a return to the shareholders. All the investors sold half of their investments. Tipps got $50,000 for stock that had cost him a bit more than $11,000. And that was only the beginning.

The company kept growing, adding posters, market research, and special-purpose magazines to its product line. In 1979 it bought *Esquire* magazine, which was nearly bankrupt, and slowly turned it around. In several corporate reorganizations over the last few years, Tipps has sold an additional 25 percent of his stock for $450,000. Valuing his remaining shares conservatively, it's realistic to say that his initial investment has increased forty-fold. And Tipps wasn't the earliest or the most successful of the 13–30 investors. At least one of the original partners in the business literally retired at age thirty-five on his profits. And I'll show you it's not as difficult as you think to find similar opportunities.

Invest in What You Know

All these people's strategies have one element in common: each person used his own personal talents and skills to recognize and create value. No successful person I've met has trusted brokers or mutual-fund companies to make money for him. And none has deliberately sought out a "hot" field where he could get rich. All have found their own investment opportunities in their own worlds.

Most people's financial strategies don't thoroughly utilize their talents and skills. Saving money in a bank certainly doesn't use your unique abilities. Neither does investing in the stock market: when you choose a stock, you're competing with thousands of professional pension-fund managers who can afford far better research facilities than yours. You add nothing to the value of the stock or to the productivity of the company behind it.

But when you buy and manage a building, create a business, or invest in the business of a friend you know to be capable, you're using your own intelligence to do something useful. Creative individual investors like Harry and Betty, Bruce Rueppel, and Maynard Tipps know and can do things in their own circles that hotshot investment professionals can't know or do. And they end up well compensated for their adventures.

In all sorts of fields — no doubt including whatever field you know well — there are many opportunities to invest or create businesses. I know a newspaperman who started a newsletter, three engineers who invested in an electronics start-up, a math teacher who set up a computer store, and a registered nurse who made some extra money on a "camp" for Cabbage Patch Kids. Children send their dolls away for two weeks for $35, receive a postcard from the doll while it's at camp, and get a group picture of their doll with other Cabbage Patch "campers" when it returns home.

A law or clinical-psychology practice is, of course, a business as well, and needs to be treated like one.

You may convert knowledge that has nothing to do with your training into value. If you simply recognize the determination of a friend who's starting a business or comprehend the virtues of a neighborhood where houses are undervalued, that's using your own personal knowledge and skills to create value as well.

Often you can start businesses part-time while doing another job during the day. I doubled a $2,000 investment in a year by giving the money to a friend who was producing a quality line of calendars. He started the business while a student at Harvard Business School and ran it in eight to fifteen hours per week while working full-time as an advertising account executive.

But although all intelligent strategies involve actively using your skills to create value, they vary enormously in risk and excitement. Harry and Betty and Bruce Rueppel made relatively safe real estate investments that were pretty much sure things. *Trillions* of dollars worth of real estate needs to be managed in the United States. Many good values almost always exist. You can be confident you'll at least come out OK — and probably do extremely well — in real estate if you just follow the strategies in this book. Other investments, like Maynard Tipps's investment in 13–30 Corp., involve far greater risk. And the people who founded the company — essentially betting five years of their lives on it — took a big gamble. 13–30 ran up $1 million in liabilities before it became solidly profitable.

You need to find a financial strategy that's right for you — that helps toward *your* goals without involving risks you can't handle.

Can You Do What You Want to Do?

This book is for people who have seen other men and women like themselves do well and yet doubt that they have the resources, savvy, or time to do the same. People like

- Bob, thirty-one, and Joan, thirty. Bob is a manager in a large corporation who earns $32,000 a year. Joan just gave birth to their first child and isn't sure she wants to go back to her old job as a librarian.
- Harry, twenty-six, a staff artist at a small ad agency who has $3,000 in savings and would like to work independently.
- John, thirty, a lawyer who is renting an apartment, has $8,000 in savings and investments and $4,000 in student loans, and wants to become a partner in the firm where he now works.
- Sheri, twenty-eight, a medical intern who has $4,000 in savings and $25,000 in student loans, but who wants to set up a medical practice with less pain than many new doctors suffer.
- Allan, thirty-eight, who manages a troubled computer store and is trying to figure out what to do next.
- Ellen, twenty-two, who's just out of school, earning $20,000 a year in the training program of a big food corporation, and doubtful that she wants to spend her life selling frozen dinners.
- Ronald, thirty-three, who's a research scientist in a large electronics corporation earning $38,000 a year. He's part of a group that occasionally flies to Las Vegas to make a few extra bucks using the card-counting strategy a friend of his invented. He owns a home and has $25,000 in cash and investments, but knows he isn't managing those resources well.
- Dick, twenty-four, a teacher who would like to remain in teaching but doesn't want to live his whole life on a teacher's salary.
- Jan, twenty-eight, an investment banker who has only $3,000 in personal investments because he doesn't save much and the hot tips he's picked up on Wall Street haven't turned out to be that hot.

- Ann, thirty-five, who is completing training in computer programming after ten years of teaching and working as a guidance counselor. Her real dream is to establish a software company that will make products to help children learn.

By the time you finish this book, I want you to be smart about money and know how to achieve whatever realistic goal you choose. You'll know

- How to map out a financial strategy appropriate for your economic and career situation today.
- How to use your knowledge to discover creative investments.
- How to choose and manage real estate so it creates big profits with minimal pain.
- How to organize and structure partnerships with your friends to use everyone's skills, minimize everyone's risks, and participate in the best kinds of deals with very little money.
- How to use leverage safely, borrowing from banks and sometimes even credit card companies to build your wealth and put assets to work better.
- How to take advantage of the tax laws in ways that are unlikely to be affected by current tax-reform plans.
- How to hire and use a banker, a lawyer, and an accountant — and how to maximize what you get from them.
- How to build a strategy around unusual career goals that may seem to make some of the best financial techniques hard to use.
- How to judge when more conventional investments and investment strategies such as purchasing stocks, bonds, and mutual funds can genuinely benefit you.

This book isn't a "complete investment guide" in the usual sense. "Complete investment guides" usually send you straight to the stock markets, and they're almost useless to most people in their twenties and thirties, when they have little to invest. Even if a guide shows how to earn 15 percent a year after taxes and inflation (a very good return), $8,000 compounded at 15 percent a year for five years is still only $16,091. That's a reasonable return, but it won't change your way of life. And very few nonprofessional investors do much better than that in the stock market over the long haul. It's common, on the other hand, for people to turn $8,000 into $50,000 or $100,000 in five years through real estate or other businesses they build or invest in on the side — often without taking big risks.

Ethics in Business

I suspect that a key reason many young people have avoided doing business on their own is that they fear they'll have to be unethical to make money. And it's true that doing business in the real world may involve you in problems you'd rather avoid. The real world contains real ethical dilemmas, and businessmen must face them every day. Being ethical in business is a big challenge: when you're in business you're suddenly forced to be realistic. It's easy to sit at a desk and say banks shouldn't evict people. When you're a property owner, you may find that if you don't evict some tenants, your property will turn into a slum — or will remain a slum if it's one already.

I admire people who have handled resources creatively and profitably and yet dealt with hardship cases reasonably, professionally, and with a willingness to sacrifice profits to make life easier for decent people in trouble. One property owner I encountered — Kit Barry, a collector and dealer in nineteenth-century commercial art who at the time was thirty-four years old — found himself owning the town slum in Brattleboro, Vermont. Rather than try to convert it to middle-income housing as he had originally planned, he wound up taking care of the people who lived there during the time he owned the building — finding a doctor who would make house calls under Medicaid, helping people who had trouble with social service agencies, and breaking up fights between drunken men and their wives or lovers. "It was a very intense five years," Barry says. "I was looking at a gun or a knife more than a few times."

Barry ultimately sold the building (at a small profit) when a state agency demanded he spend $40,000 that he didn't have on safety improvements. He's glad he spent the time on the building and the people in it, but he says that if he got into a similar situation again he would do things differently: He would hire someone else to collect the rent and get into interminable conversations with tenants rather than doing it himself. He would look for a charitable foundation to support his work with the people. And he might look for a richer person to become a limited partner and take advantage of the enormous tax write-offs that his building generated. With a limited partner benefiting from the tax write-offs, Barry could afford to pay himself a salary that would compensate, at least partially, for the efforts he was putting in as owner.

Barry is one of many good-deed-doers who over the past couple of decades have found that their efforts for good causes have been much less effective than they could have been because they didn't pay enough attention to intelligent management. It's unfortunate when good projects fall so far short of their goals for such a reason.

On the other hand, many good people have often acted as if owning buildings or starting companies was something no one as virtuous as they would ever do. But when millions of people continually tell each other that landlords are immoral, the only result is that moral people don't wind up owning buildings. And the world could use more moral people owning buildings.

This book simply urges you to seek good profits by doing things that other people want or need. It urges you to plan what you do intelligently and in a businesslike way. You don't make money instead of doing good. You do it as a necessary support for anything worthwhile.

Intelligent Risks

Any investment more adventurous than a bank account involves some risk. I'll show throughout this book how you can evaluate risks, and how the risks in investments you find for yourself are often far lower than those you could buy through a broker, such as stock options. You have to weigh risks against potential gains and build a life that is secure (as much as is possible these days), honest, and aimed at true prosperity.

Perhaps it won't be as easy for you to make hundreds of thousands of dollars in some fields — especially real estate — in the late eighties as it was for others in the seventies. The enormous inflation of the 1970s is probably behind us. But the world needs the creativity and management that you contribute when you act entrepreneurially. It pays people well for creating value. Anyone smart enough to pass a difficult college course is almost certain over a moderate period — say, four or five years — to do much better by trying to actively create wealth than if he took conventional advice and put money aside for a rainy day in bank accounts, stock market investments, or mutual funds. I think you can reach whatever goal you set in life. And in this book, I think I can show you how.

A Financial Strategy for Your Life

The first step in building any kind of strategy should be to define what you really want to do. That sounds obvious, but most personal-finance books ignore it. Think of people you admire. You'll probably realize they've succeeded because (1) they had a reasonably clear idea of what they wanted in life, and (2) they were concentrating on things they knew and probably enjoyed.

One friend of mine was a record collector. He had the largest collection of golden oldies in Los Angeles. He wanted to make a business of his passion, so he started a used-record store. He used the capital and contacts from the store to set up an independent record company that licenses hits from the 1950s and '60s from their original distributors, repackages them, and sells them all over the country. As more people buy video recorders, he's starting to distribute videos from the same era.

Another acquaintance was a photographer outside Boston. She realized she was more upset about the mediocrity of photo processing than excited about the rat race she had to go through to get photographic assignments. She created her own photo lab.

A third was a high school math teacher. He didn't necessarily want to spend his whole life in a high school, but he knew that he enjoyed teaching people how to do things. He set up one of California's first computer stores.

Are You Ready to Pick a Goal?

Think about what you want to do in life. It is very easy to get out of college and get a job and a salary (or a stream of commissions or whatever) that's more than you need. Rather than think about the possibility that you might want to raise children or establish yourself outside of the nine-to-five grind, you buy a fancy car or drop a few thousand dollars on a hot stock tip you don't really understand. (One friend of mine says he has "an uncanny sense of the stock market" — but it's 180 degrees in the wrong direction.)

Usually the best goal is the least fashionable: if everyone wants to be a college professor or a newspaperman or even a lawyer this year, then it's probably a bad time to go into those trades. In fact, if there ever occurs a year when everyone is setting out to be a real estate investor or a small-scale entrepreneur, watch out. (But good real estate managers and entrepreneurs are so much more important than lawyers that there may never be a surplus of them. The real danger is probably that particular *kinds* of real estate and entrepreneurship will become too fashionable.)

A pretty good test of whether an idea is a good business proposition is whether it's on one hand plausible enough that you can find partners willing to invest in it, and on the other hand unfashionable enough that at least some of your friends consider it an odd project to spend a lot of time on. Life goals also should be plausible enough that you can discuss them with your friends, but idiosyncratic enough that many of your friends consider you a bit unusual when they hear about them. If you really want to be a good corporate marketing manager or doctor, you'll find plenty of people who regard you as weird. But the goal that's dangerous is the goal that's so vaguely worked out that it can't shock anybody.

Try to List Your Goals

You can start working on a financial strategy even if you have no well-defined goals yet. Whatever you want to do, you'll be able to do it better with greater financial resources, and you can start building your financial resources immediately.

But it's wise to start creating a strategy by looking at your goals. You probably have a larger and more complex collection of goals than you imagine; try "brainstorming" to find out what they are. Simply sit down and write down goals as they come to mind. (A word processor may make brainstorming easier, but it's not necessary.) Don't worry about whether the goals you're listing are practical or wise — you can figure that out later. Spend about a half an hour at this, then leave and come back to the task later. After you've listed every conceivable goal in your head, go down the list and choose those that are truly central.

If you've listed radically contradictory goals, you may want to try to modify them so they are consistent. I'll try to show that even goals as seemingly contradictory as "To continue teaching public school" and "To own a large yacht" may be reconcilable; I wouldn't necessarily urge you to cross anything off your list that you genuinely want. At least not yet.

I would urge you to pick no more than five or six top goals and see if you can pursue them. Many won't last a lifetime. And if you want to go into business for yourself, you'll have to refine the assorted goals you've written down a great deal. Unless you know what goals you have and how important each one is to you, you won't be able to create a meaningful strategy for meeting them.

The Smart-Money Spiral

Once you know the extent of your goals, you can start working on a strategy to reach them. Just as your goals aren't set in concrete, your strategy too can change over time, but it makes sense to figure out what you think you should do, write it down, and revise it consciously, not accidentally.

Most intelligent strategies involve one form or another of this "Smart-Money Spiral":

1. Maximize cash flow till you encounter a chance to invest for a worthwhile profit.

It's pointless to spend much time worrying about investments when you have only a few thousand dollars in savings. Concentrate on advancing in your field and, if opportunities present themselves, on side jobs such as consulting, freelance art, or selling.

2. Look for a good deal on a piece of real estate, and invest in it when you can.

Not everyone will devote a large portion of his life to real estate, but virtually everyone should own at least some. Though stocks, bonds, and mutual funds get most publicity when the media write about investments, actually there's much more money invested in real estate and vastly more money made there. By *Forbes* magazine's calculation, the total value of all widely traded stocks (including those traded over the counter) is $1.9 trillion — not a trivial amount, but only a fraction of the money invested in real estate. The total value of residential real estate alone in the United States is $4.5 trillion.

And unlike stocks and bonds, most real estate needs a concerned individual owner who will look after it. It is in the nation's interest to encourage those owners by ensuring a decent return on their investment; otherwise, the structures of the nation would literally fall apart from neglect.

Real estate buyers do get excellent returns compared to those available in the stock market:

- Most real estate investors make large profits with manageable risk. Hundreds of thousands of people have $100,000 or more in equity on properties where they invested $5,000 or less of their own money.
- Real bargains come along in real estate more often than in any other field where you can invest.
- Owning your home can give you a fine place to live at a favorable price and with a chance to earn a big profit.
- Real estate (except vacation homes) offers overwhelming tax advantages even under expected revisions in the tax laws.
- Real estate is excellent collateral you'll be able to use if you need to borrow for further investments — or for any other purpose.

Carefully choose at least one piece of real estate, probably a home to live in. Take your time and find a bargain — a place that provides the kind of *value* you or others want, but whose price doesn't fully reflect that value, perhaps because the neighborhood isn't well-known or perhaps because the seller is particularly anxious to raise cash for some reason. New tax laws are likely to reduce the value of some real estate, especially in high-tax states like New York. Make sure that you pay a low enough price that the home you buy will remain a good deal under *any* likely tax reform. But don't let tax confusion keep you from starting an investment program.

3. After holding for a while, "flip" the asset.

If you truly love a place you've bought, you may want to spend the rest of your life there, but soon after they've bought them most people should think about selling their properties. If you've chosen your property wisely, the price you can get will probably rise over the next one to five years as others notice what a nice place you've got. Meanwhile, the value of the tax deductions you're getting will go down: as the principal of the mortgage starts to decline, you'll be paying less of your income in interest. Your income, on the other hand, should be rising as you get raises or do better in other activities. You want to realize some of the profits on your investment and also obtain bigger tax deductions.

The way to do this is to sell your property at a profit and invest in a well-chosen new asset. You should have accumulated enough equity in the property you've sold to make a down payment on a better property and still have some cash left over.

If your property doesn't increase in value, it's probably a good idea to sell it anyway. Probably you've discovered that whatever merits you saw in it did not really exist. If you still think it's a terrific place, keep it. Others may catch on eventually. But if you made a mistake, get out. And buy more carefully next time.

4. Invest the additional cash in something you understand.

Put the cash that's left over after you've moved into a better asset, either more real estate (this is the time to buy a second building, if you want to make real estate a serious sideline) or another venture such as a side business of your own, friends' businesses, or a well-thought-out program of traditional investments such as stocks and mutual funds. By this time you should have $15,000 to $30,000 to invest, and that's enough to make conventional investing worthwhile. But remember that most people can make most money with least risk by investing in things they know: if not real estate or their own businesses, then certainly other businesses they understand.

If you don't flip your first asset, keep track of how much it's worth, and borrow against it to invest in something else.

5. Keep building your resource base, but when an investment goes sour, don't be afraid to take a loss.

Everybody makes mistakes; the people who end up poor are those who won't admit it. Sometimes a recession sets in and everyone's investments go down. When that happens you should just sit tight and wait for a recovery. But occasionally a neighborhood you'd expected to improve goes downhill instead. You buy a stock in a promising industry, but the company gets clobbered by a competitor. You start a business, but you can't sell your product. Don't wait to break even. The most valuable item you'll get out of this fiasco is the experience that will keep you from making the same mistake again. Look for a good opportunity to get your money out.

Of course, there are many variations on the Smart-Money Spiral. On one hand, you may find you can invest in real estate even before you've accumulated much cash. As I'll show in the next chapter, you should take account of your borrowing power when you figure out how much you can invest. I bought a $95,000 coop when I had only $3,000 in cash. It was on a rundown Upper West Side block in Manhattan. Two blocks away, similar apartments with fresh coats of paint were worth $200,000. And developers had already begun renovating two hotels on the block. It was such a good investment that I felt I could justify a $9,000 unsecured personal loan and the borrowing of $10,000 on my credit cards. I made a profit of $3,500 in my first full year of ownership because of tax benefits I wouldn't have received if I had continued renting. And when I sold the building a year and a half after I bought it, I realized a capital gain of $75,000. Borrowing heavily to buy the place where you intend to live often makes sense for even the most cautious investor.

On the other hand, people with children won't want to flip their main asset if it's the house where they are raising their family. They'll have to work to build their cash position longer than single people, but couples also have opportunities that single people lack. One person can start a business while minding the kids, while the other works at a standard cash flow–oriented job, for example.

The variations don't change the importance of the Smart-Money Spiral, however. Whoever you are, you'll get where you want to be by maximizing cash flow till you find a good opportunity to get into real estate, then managing the profits the hard assets bring, and then investing in your own and others' businesses. If you want to take control of your life and accomplish any important goals, you need to figure out where you are on the Smart-Money Spiral and build a financial strategy around it to bring you toward your goals.

If you're renting an apartment, is it time to buy a place to live? If you own a home or another asset, is it time to move to a better one? Or is it time to start investing in a business? Or should you be using the equity in your assets to finance a move to what you'd really like to be doing with your life? How will the actions you're taking now get you to where you want to be?

The Spiral Can Work for Anyone

Some people's way of life makes planning difficult. Suppose you work for a corporation that routinely transfers people all over the world. Or suppose you're an anthropologist who must plan to live for a year or more at a time in odd corners of the world. These jobs make planning a financial strategy more complex, but not impossible.

Often, the moves forced by careers like this occur at three-to-six-year intervals — time enough to flip a property anyway. And people in these careers often face especially good opportunities to create their own businesses around their jobs: a journalist I know set up a Tokyo-based newsletter, for example. If you build on what you know, your strange way of life can be an asset in creating a financial strategy, rather than a liability. But people who know they may have to move on a few months' notice should try especially hard to build financial strategies around partnerships, as I'll discuss in chapter 4. Then if they must suddenly move to Botswana, there's someone else to mind the store and make sure nothing has to be sold at distress prices.

Become Wealthy Producing Value

The Smart-Money Spiral makes people wealthy for simple reasons: people who start out with little cash make money through hard assets and small-scale entrepreneurship because these activities put the nation's resources to use effectively. They're much more vital to prosperity than ordinary work in nine-to-five jobs. Houses and neighborhoods need to be cared for; ideas need to be transformed into productive businesses. Moreover, the government knows these jobs need to be done and has deliberately designed the tax laws to encourage people to do them.

Certainly this small-scale wheeling and dealing doesn't embody all the virtue the world needs. But it's good, constructive work. It will move you toward your goals, whatever they may be.

How Much Can You Really Afford to Invest?

Most people think they can afford to invest very little. Or they think that if they've accumulated a few thousand dollars, they should start "investing" by buying stocks or mutual fund shares — perhaps planning to make bigger investments in real estate or small businesses later when they have more money.

Actually, almost anyone with a steady job has enough resources to begin real investing if he understands his assets correctly, chooses an investment carefully, is ready to make some small short-term sacrifices, and uses leverage — the borrowing of other people's money — intelligently.

Your Balance Sheet

Take Ted, a stockbroker who feels he can't afford to own any stocks. Ted earns $30,000 a year, which comes to only $22,000 — about $420 a week — after taxes. Ted enjoys such luxuries as good food and wine, and he hasn't been able to save any money on his salary.

The first step in planning to invest is to create a simple balance sheet — a listing of major assets and liabilities. As indicated below, you'll need to give your bank a more complex balance sheet when you apply for mortgage loans, but at this point you can keep it simple. You'll only confuse matters if you list assets that you couldn't or wouldn't sell to raise investment cash.

Here's a balance-sheet form filled in with data for Ted:

ASSETS

Liquid	
Cash on hand	$ 100
Bank accounts	400
Stocks	1,100
Mutual funds	
Money market	470
Other	—
Savings bonds, travelers checks, and other readily cashable assets	—
Other	
Real estate	—
Automobile(s)	6,000
Tax refund due	—
Money owed to him	—
Cash value of life-insurance policies	—
Business equipment (computer, type-writer, etc.)	—
Any interest in a small business	—
Retirement plans	
IRA	—
Vested interest in an employer plan	—
Other	—
TOTAL ASSETS	**$8,070**

AVAILABLE LINES OF CREDIT

MasterCard	$1,500
Visa: Bank A	2,000
Visa: Bank B	2,800
American Express (Gold Card)	3,000

LIABILITIES

Car loan	$1,600
MasterCard	800

Visa: Bank A	1,300
Visa: Bank B	1,400
Bills due	340
Taxes due	—
Personal loans	—
Mortgages	—
Education loans	—
Other loans	—
Other liabilities	—
TOTAL LIABILITIES	$5,440

This does not seem promising. Ted's credit card debts exceed the value of his stocks by some $2,400. What little net worth this listing shows is tied up in his car, which is rapidly depreciating. Moreover, when Ted adds up his expenses, he finds they exceed his after-tax income. This doesn't surprise him, because he has found he's never able to pay off his credit card balances. Here are Ted's expenses:

Expense	Monthly	Yearly
Rent	$500	$ 6,000
Telephone	30	360
Electricity/gas	35	420
Cable TV	15	180
Credit card interest payments	180	2,160
Car	100	1,200
Car insurance	—	600
Clothing (average)	180	2,160
Dry cleaning	25	300
Laundry	10	120
Food and wine (at home)	350	4,200
Outside meals	200	2,400
Other entertainment	160	1,920
Gifts	—	500

Expense	Monthly	Yearly
Donations	—	500
Vacations	—	1,200
TOTAL EXPENSES		$24,220

Obviously there are parts of this list that could be cut in an emergency. But Ted is comfortable living a bit dangerously, and the purpose of money management is to allow you to live as you want to live and accomplish your life goals, not to continually cut your budget in order to meet somebody's arbitrary definition of fiscal prudence. Ted may have to cut his spending or move to a slightly less desirable home as a short-term tactic to launch his investment program, but he doesn't want to cut his budget aggressively, and I don't think he has to. (On the other hand, I *don't* think people should push to spend more than they feel comfortable spending on their current income, and other people in Ted's situation might want to economize more than I'll suggest for Ted.)

What an Investment Can Do for Ted

Many experts believe a person in Ted's position should invest his time in his profession and quickly try to raise his income to $35,000 to $40,000 a year. *Then* he could start investing. And that's a perfectly reasonable strategy for someone like Ted.

But it's important to realize that Ted can start a genuine investment program within a few months, if he chooses. His immediate goal should be to buy a home whose value he can increase. If he handles the purchase well, he'll be able to flip the place — that is, sell it and buy another and liberate $10,000 to $50,000 in the process — within a year and a half or so.

The process is fairly simple and doesn't involve any remarkable shenanigans. Ted probably must buy a condominium to get a place he can afford and can improve without effort that will detract from his job. He should look for a poorly cared for condo in a nice building in a good — preferably improving — location.

Ted's current, $500-a-month place is near the beach in San Diego. With careful searching, he can probably find an equally well located — but poorly cared for — one-bedroom condominium for $70,000 or so that would be worth perhaps $85,000 if it were in better condition. He's looking for a seller who wants to get rid of his home quickly for some reason — maybe he's been transferred to a job in another city. If Ted finds he can't handle the down payment and monthly costs of a $70,000 purchase, he may have to settle for something a little farther from the beach — say, a $55,000 condo that will be worth $68,000 when properly marketed.

The idea is to fix up the property and put it on the market again, taking the time necessary to sell it at a good price. That should produce a large profit on little cash investment.

Say Ted finds a $70,000 condo that he thinks would be worth $90,000 if cleaned up. He can probably arrange for a floating-rate mortgage that will cover 85 percent of the purchase price, or $59,500. He'll have to put up a down payment of $10,500, but I'll suggest several strategies below that can help him find this money even if he has little cash.

Now suppose real estate prices rise only 6 percent over the next year and a half in the neighborhood Ted has chosen. Ted has paid $500 (perhaps borrowed from a credit card company) to some painting contractors to improve his place. He may also have paid to have a kitchen appliance repaired and replaced a bathroom mirror himself. His condominium is now much more desirable, and he can now put it on the market, asking $98,000. He'll "settle" for $90,000.

Here's how Ted will use the $90,000:

Sale price	$90,000
Costs of sale (brokerage fee or other)	(5,400)
Net sale price	$84,600
Repayment to bank	(59,500)
Proceeds to Ted	25,100
Repayment of credit card debt used for improvements	(1,000)
Available cash	$24,100

If Ted has borrowed the whole $10,500 for the down payment, he'll probably repay some of that, too — say $5,000. He still has $19,100 left over. He can put $12,000 down on a better condominium and still have $7,100 left over for any purpose he chooses.

And that's what happens if things go only modestly well. If Ted has chosen his $70,000 property really well, it could increase in value to $125,000 or so. Then he can sell the property, repay the bank and the cost of improvements, and have approximately $58,000 left over. If he then buys another property for $125,000 with an 85 percent mortgage, he'll have over $39,000 in available cash.

Why Careful Home-Buying Is So Profitable

If this seems like magic to you, reread the last few paragraphs carefully. These first steps on the Smart-Money Spiral have made more people comfortable — and more people rich — than all the stocks on Wall Street put together.

When you take these steps, you're taking responsibility for managing both a piece of property and the money you've borrowed from the bank. When you choose a property that's in disrepair, you're fixing up the management failures of the guy who owned it before you. And by paying interest to the bank, you're giving the lenders a decent return on their money without work or significant risk on their part.

When you rent, on the other hand, you're paying other people to manage property and money for you. A big management fee is built into your rent payments. Paying someone to manage for you is wasteful, because you can ordinarily take care of your home more efficiently than a landlord. But even putting aside the waste involved, the amount you pay is just too high. Monthly real estate payments may look higher than rent, but actually they are largely investments. You get money back when you sell or refinance your property.

Only a couple of warnings are necessary:

First, *condominiums are riskier investments than other types of real estate because the market is less mature.* People are still unsure how to value a condominium in many parts of the country. Some people have bought condominiums for $40,000 and sold them for $400,000. Others have bought condominiums for $90,000 only to watch their value fall to $60,000 — wiping out their entire down payment and more.

Condominium disasters most commonly occur when a builder or a whole group of builders launch developments but can't sell all the units at the price they wanted. The unsalable units may be dumped on the market at a loss. Cheap construction techniques compound the problems. People who bought when the units first became available — no doubt dazzled by promises of tax benefits and capital gains — suddenly find that their property is worth far less than they paid.

These disasters emphasize the key principle that Ted and all other real estate investors should be following anyway: only buy a property that provides real, long-term, after-tax *value* to you. That means a good place to live at a reasonable after-tax cost. *Never* buy something only because you're promised its price will rise. If a property is valuable to you, it will be valuable to others and its price will go up. But prices rise only if value is there. If a property *isn't* valuable to you, it won't be valuable to anyone else.

Second, *new tax laws could cut the value of many properties.* You can still count on well-chosen real estate being a good investment in the long run. But if, when you calculate the value of a property to you, you assume that you'll continue to get the tax benefits the government is abolishing, you can wind up paying too much. Be sure to find a bargain. I'll give more advice on how to do that in chapter 5.

Monthly Mortgage Payments Are Easy to Handle

Ted may find that financing a home is tough, but he can do it even without accumulating savings in advance. Banks simply care about making sure their loan will be repaid, and Ted has enough income to repay a loan.

At first glance it may look like Ted faces two serious problems:

- finding the down payment, and
- handling monthly mortgage and condominium maintenance payments significantly higher than his rent.

Actually, only the down payment will be a problem. Ted's monthly mortgage and condominium maintenance costs may *look* high. Typically a mortgage for someone in Ted's position will cover 75 to 90 percent of the cost of a home. For a $70,000 condominium, an 85 percent mortgage would amount to $59,500. A $59,500, thirty-year, 10.5 percent floating-rate mortgage will require monthly payments of about $545. Condominium maintenance charges will add another $150 or so. That's a total of $695 a month.

But actually, that $695 is likely to cost Ted about the same as his current $500 a month rent. Here's how:

In 1985, Ted was in the 30 percent federal income-tax bracket. He was also in the 8 percent bracket for California state income tax. Home-mortgage interest payments were fully deductible on both federal and state tax returns (and will continue to be deductible under virtually all proposed tax "reforms"). Thus for every dollar of interest paid, Ted would save almost 35 cents in taxes. (You can't simply add 8 percent to 30 percent to calculate the savings because — at least through 1985 — local taxes have been deductible on federal tax forms. Thus every dollar of local tax savings increases Ted's federal taxes.)

Of Ted's $545 monthly mortgage payment, roughly $520 will be interest in the first years. Thus the condominium purchase will save Ted some $175 a month in taxes, and its net cost will be nearly the same as the $500 a month he's paying now. (See Example 1.) And the tax savings of home ownership would remain substantial under any tax simplification plan currently proposed.

Moreover, any employee buying a property can immediately increase his monthly cash flow to cover the carrying costs by filing a new W-4 tax form with his employer.

Everyone fills out a W-4 form when he starts work. It asks you how many tax *exemptions* should be assumed in calculating the federal income tax that will be withheld from your pay. The more exemptions you list, the less tax your employer will withhold.

The form comes with a worksheet that advises you to take one exemption for yourself and one for each dependent (kids, a non-working spouse, etc.), but legally you can and should ignore the worksheet when you own a home or have other important tax deductions. You want to list the number of exemptions that will produce a small refund for you and give you enough cash to live on and invest through the year.

Try taking one exemption for every $1,000 a year in mortgage interest you will be paying. Legally, you can take up to fourteen exemptions without the Internal Revenue Service even being notified, and you can take even more if you can explain to the IRS why you thought they wouldn't cause you to owe any money at the end of the year.

If Ted fills out a new W-4 form showing more exemptions, he can handle $675 a month in condominium payments easier than he's now handling $500 in rent.

EXAMPLE 1: How Ted can finance a $70,000 condo with only $1,500 in available cash

Purchasing costs

Condo price	$70,000
Less 85% financing	(59,500)
Down payment needed	10,500
Bank points (2 points)	1,200
Legal fees, etc.	600
TOTAL CASH NEEDED	$12,300

Sources of Funds

Personal liquid assets	$ 1,500
Personal loan	5,000
Credit cards or loan from seller	5,800
TOTAL FUNDS	$12,300

Monthly Costs	Before Tax	Tax Benefits in First Year**	Net Cost after Tax
Bank mortgage*	545	175	370
Condo maintenance	150	0	150
Personal loan (4 years at 15%)	140	21	119
Credit cards or second mortgage	260	30	230
Bank points	0***	35	(35)
TOTAL	$1,095	$261	$834

Ted's monthly payments, after taxes, will be $834.

---

*Floating rate; first year at 10½% interest; over thirty years
**Assumes 35% total marginal tax bracket
***$1,200 in bank points were paid up front and are fully deductible; therefore there is no monthly cost, but there is an annual tax benefit of $420. For this analysis, I am showing it as $35 per month.

Credit Strategy and Ted's Down Payment

Ted's real problem — one that may seem insurmountable — will be coming up with the $10,500 for a down payment when he only has $2,070 in liquid assets. He'll have to borrow all or most of the down payment in addition to taking out a mortgage.

The need to borrow the down payment may cause Ted to buy a cheaper home, but it shouldn't force him to remain a renter. Because Ted has held a good job for more than a year and has only a few thousand dollars in debt, he's very creditworthy. If he carefully approaches the many credit sources available to him, he can almost certainly put together the money he needs to buy an apartment.

I think everyone should have a *credit strategy* at all times. Always have an answer to the question: "If I needed to borrow an amount equal to half my annual salary on an unsecured basis right now, how would I do it?"

If Ted, who's now twenty-six, had been more careful about developing credit lines from the time he left school, he probably wouldn't have any trouble borrowing $10,500 today. He might choose not to do it, because the most readily available credit sources would require him to pay $300–$400 a month to cover an additional $10,500 in debt. But the choice would be his, not a bank's.

Try to think about yourself as a banker does. Banks commonly use rules of thumb to decide whether consumers are creditworthy. One rule used in some areas says that consumers can't afford to pay more than 40 percent of their pretax income in debt service — the principal and interest on loans. That's quite a lot; for Ted it would come to $12,000 a year, or $1,000 a month.

In addition to keeping debt service below 40 percent of income, however, banks require that each individual loan or increase in a credit card limit have its own justification. Ted can't simply walk into a bank and expect to borrow $30,000 for three years, even though he could repay it at $1,000 a month or so. The bank wants to know that the reason for Ted's borrowing is good or — in the case of a line of credit such as credit cards provide — that Ted's past behavior indicates he can be trusted with the money.

Developing Lines of Credit

Try to develop significant *credit lines* — commitments from financial institutions that they'll lend to you whenever you want.

Banks are delighted to give out credit cards with medium-sized credit lines attached. If you're creditworthy, they're delighted to give out cards with lines as large as $5,000. Credit card lending is highly profitable because the interest rate is high and there's little overhead. That's why you get so much junk mail from banks asking you to apply for cards. And possessing significant credit lines greatly increases your financial flexibility.

If you've regularly paid your bills, nothing is easier than raising the credit limit on cards you already possess. Simply write a letter to the bank that issued the card and tell them you love the card but you'll have to do business with other banks if they won't raise the limit to the amount you want.

But don't take out cards from a dozen banks, even though you could theoretically get credit lines of $20,000 to $30,000 that way. And be careful not to take out credit cards from stores where you don't regularly shop. When banks calculate whether you've got too much credit, they add in not only the loans you've actually taken out, but also all the money you *would* have outstanding if you ran up all your credit lines to the maximum.

Instead of randomly applying for credit cards whenever some bank sends an application at a convenient time, concentrate on a few "premium" cards with credit lines of $5,000 or so each. One good strategy is to seek three credit cards: an American Express Gold Card, a Premium Visa or MasterCard from a large national bank, and a Visa or MasterCard with as high a limit as possible from a local bank. I maintain credit lines equal to one-fourth my annual income. When I need to borrow more than that, I take out a personal loan at a lower interest rate than the credit card companies charge.

Some large banks also have special credit-line plans that carry lower interest rates than credit cards. These allow you to write checks for a loan. They are extremely worthwhile. The banks send applications to creditworthy people, often with an announcement that you've been preapproved for a credit line of a few thousand dollars and you're welcome to apply for a larger one. Accept these credit lines if they're offered to you.

A banker will think you're businesslike if you maintain a few large credit lines. But how can you explain an array of low-limit bank cards? They make you look disorganized and unbusinesslike, and in fact they encourage you to *be* disorganized and unbusinesslike. How does Ted keep track of the balances on four different cards?

If you have a $5,000 line of credit from a national bank — or if you've received a letter offering you a $5,000 card — try going to your local bank and telling them you'll do most of your business through them if they'll just raise your limit to the same amount the national bank will give. It's a reasonable request, and if the bank is well run, they'll probably do it. It's a good idea to follow through on your promise at least partially, because building relationships with local banks will be useful in the future, and problems with local banks are often a good deal easier to sort out than problems with credit card offices in Delaware or South Dakota.

Finally, keep track of what's going into the credit files that banks maintain on you. Don't apply for loans or credit cards that you probably won't get. (That means you should avoid applying for a loan or credit line when you've just changed jobs or when the new credit would bring your potential for getting into debt close to the 40-percent-of-income ceiling.) And it's a good idea to check every six months or so what's in your credit files. The nation's central credit-reporting service is TRW. Request a copy of TRW's files on you by writing them. (The address is TRW, P.O. Box 271, Parsippany, NJ 07054.) If anything is inaccurate, the credit bureau is required to change it. Credit bureaus do charge you for this service. The cost is $10 to check your TRW credit file unless you've recently been refused credit due to one of their reports. (Then they'll give you a copy of your file for free.) Checking your file is well worth the cost.

If Ted had developed credit lines carefully, it would be entirely reasonable for him to run them up to cover a large share of his down payment.

Other Sources of Down-Payment Cash

Ted probably wouldn't want to put his whole down payment on credit cards even if the banks would let him. Credit card interest rates are too high for that. So Ted should also consider these other ways to cover his down payment: *personal loans, a second mortgage taken by the seller, borrowing from family or friends, credit unions, builder financing,* and *sharing a place.*

Personal Loans   One of the simplest sources is a personal loan from a bank or other financial institution. With $30,000 in annual income, a good credit history, only about $5,500 in outstanding debt including a secured car loan, and unused credit lines of just $6,000 or so, Ted ought to qualify for a personal loan of $4,000 to $6,000 on just his own signature.

Personal loan rates and terms vary substantially from bank to bank. Often the banks with the best deals on mortgages aren't the banks with the best deals on personal loans. (Anyway, Ted shouldn't try to take out his personal loan from the bank that will be providing the mortgage.)

If Ted seeks a personal loan, he should go to a large commercial bank that will simply apply a computer-generated formula to his application, rather than to a small bank where the person who interviews him will actually be making the loan decision. He'll have to explain his purpose briefly on the loan application, and perhaps to an employee of the bank as well ("debt consolidation" — paying off debts on your credit cards and to your family — is a truthful explanation). At a large bank Ted probably won't be pressed for details. If any bank employee suggests his loan might be imprudent, he should just go to another bank.

Even the combination of credit cards and a personal loan probably shouldn't be used to cover the whole of a down payment on a $70,000 condo. Borrowing $10,500 from these short-term sources could add as much as $400 to his monthly payments and raise the total after-tax cost of his deal to as much as $834 a month. (See Example 1.) But for the down payment on a $50,000 condo, credit cards and a personal loan might be fine. (See Example 2.)

There are other ways Ted can raise a down payment, however:

A Second Mortgage Taken by the Seller If Ted's getting 80 percent of his money from the bank, he can ask the seller to accept 90 percent cash and a mortgage note for the remaining 10 percent. This is fairly common in California, less so in some other parts of the country. If a seller is anxious to move, however, he may be willing to take a second mortgage even if the practice isn't common in your area.

Borrowing from Family or Friends Most young people are too reluctant to borrow from their parents. But who else knows what a reliable person you are? Throughout history people have relied

EXAMPLE 2: How Ted can finance a $50,000 condo with only $1,500 in available cash

Purchasing costs

Condo price	$50,000
Less 85% financing	(42,500)
Down payment needed	7,500
Bank points (2 points)	850
Legal fees, etc.	600
TOTAL CASH NEEDED	$ 8,950

Sources of Funds

Personal liquid assets	$ 1,500
Personal loan	5,000
Credit cards or loan from seller	2,450
TOTAL FUNDS	$ 8,950

Monthly Costs	Before Tax	Tax Benefits in First Year**	Net Cost after Tax
Bank mortgage*	380	130	250
Condo maintenance	150	0	150
Personal loan (4 years at 15%)	140	21	119
Credit cards or second mortgage	140	13	127
Bank points	0	25	(25)
TOTAL	$810	$189	$621

Ted's monthly payments, after taxes, will be $621.

*Floating rate; first year at 10½% interest; over thirty years
**Assumes 35% total marginal tax bracket

on their families for help setting themselves up in life. And your family is likely to give you much more favorable repayment terms than your credit card company. Also, family members may be willing to simply invest in your house — giving you money in exchange for a portion of your profits.

Credit Unions Many company credit unions will lend for almost any purpose and allow longer repayment terms than banks. Often, they don't even report your loan to credit bureaus, so they don't affect your ability to borrow from other sources.

In addition, Ted should consider two other possibilities:

Builder Financing Some builders will arrange up to 95 percent financing for people like Ted. Never buy a property only because of the financing — that's how many people have wound up owning condominiums worth significantly less than the amount of their mortgage. Ted should visit at least half a dozen properties that don't offer special financing before he concludes that sellers offering good financing deals are also offering properties with good value. If they are, he should take one. It will be a lot easier to pay back a 95 percent mortgage over twenty-five to thirty years than to pay back the credit card companies as quickly as they will expect their money.

Sharing a Place Ted can buy a two-bedroom condominium, either by himself (renting out the spare room) or together with someone else. If he brings in a partner for an $82,000 condominium, he'll only need a down payment of $6,150, and his monthly costs after taxes will amount to significantly less than he's now paying. (See Example 3.) But of course his chance at profit will be less, too. See the next chapter for details on how to organize a partnership.

Ted may even be able to buy a whole two-bedroom apartment himself with hardly any more problems about a down payment than a smaller place would require. If a room in the apartment would normally rent for $300 a month, he can ask a tenant to pay him $3,000 in advance in exchange for a year's rental. That will more than cover the difference between the down payment for a $70,000 one-bedroom condo and an $82,000 two-bedroom condo. And a two-bedroom apartment is potentially a much more profitable investment than a one-bedroom.

Financial Steps for Ted

Unfortunately, Ted has never developed a credit strategy. He has to start almost from scratch. Trying to build lines of credit at this

EXAMPLE 3: How Ted can finance a shared $82,000 condo with only $1,500 in available cash

Purchasing costs

Condo price	$82,000
Less 85% financing	(69,700)
Down payment needed	12,300
Bank points (2 points)	1,400
Legal fees, etc.	600
TOTAL CASH NEEDED	$14,300
Ted's share	7,150

Sources of Funds

Personal liquid assets	$ 1,500
Personal loan	5,000
Credit cards	650
TOTAL FUNDS	$ 7,150

Monthly Costs	Before Tax	Tax Benefits in First Year**	Net Cost after Tax
Bank mortgage*	320	107	213
Condo maintenance	75	0	75
Personal loan (4 years at 15%)	140	21	119
Credit cards	54	3	51
Bank points	0	20	(20)
TOTAL	$589	$151	$438

Ted's monthly payments, after taxes, will be $438.

*Floating rate; first year at 10½% interest; over thirty years
**Assumes 35% total marginal tax bracket

point could slow him down a great deal. He should immediately request an increase in at least one credit line, but he should also start exploring other financing options. And his first step in doing that is to begin talking to potential mortgage lenders. He needs to know exactly how much of a down payment he'll require before he can put together a strategy that will produce it.

First, Ted should pay down all, or at least most, of his credit card lines. This may involve some short-term sacrifice in his life-style, but it will be worth it. Though bankers can allow up to 40 percent of your pretax income to cover debt service, having little credit card debt actually outstanding makes you *look* responsible. If Ted can't pay all his credit card debt down, he should at least pay down some and consolidate the rest on one card.

Now it's time to start visiting banks. Ted should be honest with bankers while remembering the image he wants to portray. Perhaps he should write down exactly what he wants to communicate to the banker: he's a reliable young man just starting out, who has a limited amount of cash and who wants to buy a $70,000 to $75,000 condominium. He's trying to find out how much of a down payment he must come up with and what kind of terms he can expect.

Ted should start with a goal. Perhaps

- a floating rate mortgage
- for 85 percent of the cost of his property,
- with an initial interest rate about 3 percent above the current rate for U.S. Treasury bills (listed every day in the *New York Times* and *Wall Street Journal*),
- with an interest rate "cap" so that the monthly payments can't suddenly rise by more than $100–$150 if interest rates rise, and
- minimal "points" — the fee for originating the loan. (You must plan on $600 or so in other "closing costs," such as legal fees for drawing up and registering a deed, but the "points" charged vary enormously from bank to bank.)

Ted may modify his goal as he talks to various bankers. Probably the most important part of these interviews is asking exactly how likely it is that a particular bank will give the loan he wants. In some small savings and loan institutions, Ted will wind up talking to one person who makes all the loan decisions. If Ted impresses that person that he is the sort of person who repays his debts, he may be able to count on an 80 percent or even 85 percent mortgage for whatever size property he and the banker agree is appropriate. In other institutions, on the other hand, the banker will have little power and will be evasive when asked the likelihood that a loan will be granted.

Ted must provide a balance sheet when he fills out a mortgage application that's much more elaborate than the simple listing I showed earlier. He should plan to show everything that could conceivably be considered an asset — furniture, coins given him by his grandmother, money owed him by other people, any bonus money that will be due him anytime soon from his company, and so on. The idea is to show as high a net worth as he can justify.

If Ted acts carefully, he can own a *real* investment in a few months.

Strategies for a Couple in New York City

Other people's investment needs differ from Ted's. Take Nelson and Jane, a couple living in Manhattan. They've just had their first child, a daughter named Martha. Nelson, who's twenty-seven, earns $55,000 a year as a middle manager in a large publishing company. Jane, who's twenty-six, earned $17,000 a year as a teacher in a private school until their child was born. After taxes, the two jobs together came to only $44,000. And living in the city kept them from accumulating much savings even before the baby was born.

Nelson keeps track of their balance sheet using Lotus 1-2-3 on a computer at the office where he works. Here's a modified version of his balance sheet:

ASSETS	
Liquid	
Cash on hand	$ 92
Bank accounts	
Checking	29
Money market	5,562
Savings bank	1,150
Stocks	—
Mutual funds	
Money market	—
Other	—

Savings bonds, travelers checks, and other readily cashable assets	—
Other	
Real estate	—
Automobile(s)	—
Tax refund due	2,000
Money owed to them	—
Cash value of life-insurance policies	967
Business equipment (computer, typewriter, etc.)	—
Any interest in a small business	—
Retirement plans	
IRA	6,778
Vested interest in an employer plan	3,699
Other	—
TOTAL ASSETS	**$20,277**

AVAILABLE LINES OF CREDIT

American Express Gold Card Credit Line	$5,000
Premium Visa	5,000
MasterCard A	1,500
MasterCard B	2,800
Visa: Bank A	2,000
Visa: Bank B	2,800
Visa: Bank C	1,800
Nelson's company credit union	8,000

LIABILITIES

American Express: current	$ 157
American Express Credit Line	1,050
MasterCard A	410

MasterCard B	1,613
Premium Visa	4,338
Visa: Bank A	1,522
Visa: Bank B	534
Visa: Bank C	402
Bills due	1,011
Taxes due	—
Personal loan	—
Mortgages	—
Education loan	—
Other loans	—
Other liabilities	—

TOTAL LIABILITIES $11,037

Lotus 1-2-3 hasn't helped Nelson and Jane get ahead — at least not yet. Their liquid savings (which consist largely of money Nelson had received as a bonus just before this balance sheet was prepared) are several thousand dollars less than their credit card debt. Unless they find some new sources of wealth within the next few years, they'll have to move out of Manhattan, send their child to a school they won't like, or drastically curtail their way of living when baby Martha gets old enough to need schooling.

Nelson and Jane also need tax shelter. Their combined federal, state, and city tax bracket is 44 percent — in other words, these governments will take 44 cents of every additional dollar in income they earn above their current taxable income. The new baby and Jane's temporary retirement will reduce their bracket a bit this year, but tax savings are still vital for them. Yet there's no reason why they should leave their current apartment, which at $600 a month is a bargain.

Nelson and Jane have two choices: either they can invest in some real estate they'll rent out, or they — particularly Jane, who's now home most days — can start a business.

They can't afford to own a building in Manhattan, but they can afford to buy a very nice condominium apartment or a building in another borough. Because Manhattan rents are outrageous, they can charge $1,500 a month for a condo that they can buy for

$100,000, for instance. Finding a $20,000 down payment may be a challenge, but their balance sheet is relatively strong. And they can borrow much of the money from Nelson's company credit union.

(They'll want to watch out for tax-reform proposals that would limit the amount of interest people can deduct for loans other than those that pay for their own homes. But tax proposals as this is written indicate that Nelson and Jane will surely be able to deduct $5,000 each, and that can produce as much as $4,400 a year in tax savings for the two of them. They can still get ahead by investing in real estate, but they *should* take tax-reform plans carefully into account in their buying.)

A Kindergarten Teacher

If your job doesn't put you anywhere near "a fast track," you probably need intelligent asset management even more than Ted, Nelson, and Jane. Either you want to get *on* the fast track, or you like what you're doing and you want a way to keep doing it while living a decent life.

Take Ann, for instance, a thirty-year-old kindergarten teacher near Philadelphia. Ann loves teaching, but she's thinking of giving it up. She makes $17,200 a year. After taxes that's $13,000. And she fears she'll never be able to live a decent life as long as she earns that kind of wage.

Ann has more cash than you might expect. Her balance sheet looks like this:

ASSETS

Liquid	
Cash on hand	$ 56
Bank accounts	
Checking	600
Money market	4,000
Stocks	—
Mutual funds	
Money market	—
Other	—

Savings bonds, travelers checks, and other readily cashable assets	—
Other	
Real estate	—
Automobile(s)	3,000
Tax refund due	—
Money owed to her	—
Cash value of life-insurance policies	—
Business equipment (computer, type-writer, etc.)	—
Any interest in a small business	—
Retirement plans	
IRA	2,000
Vested interest in an employer plan	—
Other	—
TOTAL ASSETS	**$9,656**

AVAILABLE LINES OF CREDIT

MasterCard	900

LIABILITIES

MasterCard	—
Bills due	200
Taxes due	—
Personal loan	—
Mortgages	—
Education loan	—
Other loans	—
Other liabilities	—
TOTAL LIABILITIES	**$200**

Ann, as you can guess by looking at her balance sheet, is very uncomfortable with debt. In fact, despite her poor-paying job, she has the strongest balance sheet and probably the highest net worth of anyone we've looked at so far. Of course, her net worth still isn't very much, but she should start out by recognizing that it's relatively high for someone who owns no real estate.

Ann's situation is common. Often people who don't care about getting on the fast track care deeply about staying out of debt. Ann's problem is how to build a good life without forcing herself to do anything she's uncomfortable with.

Ann isn't at all happy about her finances. She just can't enjoy living on $13,000 a year. Auto insurance takes fully $1,000 annually in Philadelphia. She shares a house with four other people, keeping her monthly rent to $250, but she still feels she's barely scraping by. She's taking computer courses and thinking about changing jobs, even though she loves teaching and is a good teacher.

Ann shouldn't quit teaching. She has assets that allow her to build a good life and still continue the career where her talents lie.

As a teacher, Ann has spare time — especially, but not exclusively, in the summer. Even if she doesn't want to take on any debt, she should be able to turn her spare time into wealth.

The simplest course is to join with one or two housemates and buy a house. Obviously, with Ann's very limited cash flow, she doesn't want to take out big personal loans. But anyone with $9,000 in net worth should be able to come up with $6,000 to $10,000 as a contribution to a down payment. Three such people should be able to afford a $100,000 house. If they choose carefully, they'll each have an extra $10,000 or more in net worth within a couple of years.

Ann should *stop* putting money into her Individual Retirement Account. Taxes take only 23 percent of her marginal income. When banks tell Ann she can save $460 in taxes by putting $2,000 into an IRA, that sounds like a lot. But actually $460 is trivial compared to the amount she could make by investing in a house or a part-time business. And though Ann *can* take money out of her Individual Retirement Account before she reaches age 60 — and some people can profit even after paying penalties by putting money in an IRA now and taking it out later (see chapter 10) — no one is likely to come out much ahead by putting money in an IRA at a time when their tax bracket is only 23 percent.

Ann should request a larger credit line on her charge card. Someday she may need $2,000 for something. She may also want to take out another card from another bank if she's thinking of going into business on the side. A second credit card can help her keep tax-deductible business costs separate from her ordinary charge-card expenses.

But Ann shouldn't try to go against her normal debt-averse nature. What she *should* do is try to build some real value in her spare time.

Ann says her kids' parents pressure her to use more computers in the kindergarten curriculum — where she thinks they're inappropriate. But she does think they're appropriate as a special activity for children, especially for older ones. Why not start after-school and summer programs in computer education? Only fifty kids at $30 a month will produce a cash flow of $1,500, and she can make much more than that in the summer.

Real-estate brokerage would be an even easier business to enter. If Ann doesn't want to borrow and invest money in real estate immediately, she can still become a broker with just a little training. Many senior brokers would welcome her on their staffs because she is smart and interested in people. Brokering may produce little or no cash flow until she makes her first sale. But a broker's job — helping people figure out what home will serve them well — benefits people and would use Ann's concern for others.

Thus there are many ways Ann can create value without ceasing to teach.

Strategies for a Homeowner

Many homeowners neglect their assets as much as renters. Perhaps the consequences won't be nearly so bad for them — homeowners' net worth usually increases even if they don't think about it. But unless avoiding financial entanglements is an exceptionally high priority, you should manage your assets just as aggressively when they consist of the equity in a home as when they consist of nothing but your skills and your borrowing power. Neglecting assets worth $60,000 is, if anything, worse than neglecting assets worth $6,000.

Take James, a twenty-four-year-old advertising executive in Chicago. James has been investing in mutual funds ever since he was a kid delivering newspapers, so he had no trouble buying a $55,000 condominium, paying $13,500 down. He's put $8,000 in improvements into it, and now it's worth $90,000. Here's his balance sheet:

ASSETS

Liquid

Cash on hand	$ 150
Bank accounts	3,000
Stocks	—
Mutual funds	
Money market	2,000
Other	6,000
Savings bonds, travelers checks, and other readily cashable assets	300

Other

Real estate	90,000
Automobile(s)	—
Tax refund due	—
Money owed to him	—
Cash value of life-insurance policies	—
Business equipment (computer, typewriter, etc.)	—
Any interest in a small business	—
Retirement Plans	—
IRA	
Vested interest in an employer plan	
Other	—

TOTAL ASSETS	$101,450

AVAILABLE LINE OF CREDIT

MasterCard	$500

LIABILITIES

MasterCard	—
Bills due	300
Taxes due	—

Personal loan	—
Mortgages	40,000
Education loan	—
Other loans	—
Other liabilities	—
TOTAL LIABILITIES	**$40,300**

James doesn't think of himself as rich, but he is, at least modestly. And though mutual funds were a smart investment for a student managing the money he'd saved from summer jobs, they don't use all the creativity James can muster as an adult. He should do something better with his worldly goods than leave them in mutual funds and unrealized property gains.

James should put his wealth to work. His first step is to look closely at his home equity and decide what he wants to do with it. Does he really like his current home? Is its value likely to increase rapidly in the future, or has it peaked? (You can judge that its value will increase further if there's still a great deal of renovation under way in the neighborhood, and the area is still in the process of being "discovered.")

If the home's price rise has peaked and James isn't emotionally attached to it, he should flip it for another property that he can help to increase in value. And if he wants to stay where he is, it's time for James to look for other investments. James is perfectly positioned to invest in the start-up businesses of his friends. He should increase his credit lines. (Sometimes investments come along and you don't want to sell your mutual funds.) And he should recognize that he can borrow another $40,000 at extremely favorable rates against his home.

Do You Need a Budget?

All this should show that investing is not necessarily a matter of scrimping and saving. Careful saving can be important: thrift is the largest reason James is ahead of Ted right now. But misers stay poor. People really can spend and grow rich.

How carefully should you budget your money? Personally, I've never made a careful budget for my personal life. I just try to live within my means and invest when I see the chance. Others — including most people with young children — find they need a budget.

The main point isn't whether you need to use a budget or not, it's whether you know where you stand at all times. Some people keep track of where every penny goes and yet don't have any idea how much investable cash they could raise if an opportunity presented itself. They're just giving themselves useless work.

Do a balance sheet first. What kinds of assets and liabilities do you have? *Then* think about your income and expenses. Try to list where your income over the last month went under the following categories:

Rent/mortgage/condo maintenance
Telephone
Electricity/gas/oil/water
Cable TV
Car: gas
     repairs
     insurance
     loan payments
Other interest and loan payments
Food and wine (at home)
Outside meals
Other entertainment
Culture (books, courses, etc.)
Clothing
Services (cleaning, home repairs, etc.)
Medical
Gifts (to friends and relatives)
Donations (to charities)
Other
Savings (or withdrawal from savings)
Investments

Look at these numbers. Are you satisfied with them? Or are donations, savings, and investments too low? (The national average for tax-deductible donations, incidentally, is approximately 2.3 percent of personal income.) If you feel too much is going to the wrong places, then you need a budget. Create one. If not, don't worry about it.

You *can* afford to invest. Whatever you do, however, make sure you're *investing,* or preparing to invest, in the achievement of your goals in life. You can probably do that even if you haven't yet balanced income and outgo.

Partnerships

A slick-sounding guy called me last year and said he wanted to be my "financial adviser." You know the type: a sort of upscale version of the guys who used to sell life insurance door-to-door.

I was flattered that anyone would think he could make money advising me about my finances. I pointed out that I did not have any money. That didn't matter, he said. He wanted to develop "a stable of clients" he could "grow with."

So we got together to discuss my options.

"I've got something perfect for you," he said. For $15,000 cash I could buy the depreciation tax breaks generated by one New York City bus. I would get a write-off of several times my investment. I pointed out that I didn't have $15,000. And I wouldn't want to invest in a New York City bus anyway. Though my taxes are high and will remain high under currently proposed tax reforms (as I'll indicate in chapter 10), at my stage in life I want more than just tax benefits from my investments. I want to be creating wealth, so I'll get real money back.

My "financial adviser" told me about several other possibilities that I unfortunately did not qualify for. Most of them required a net worth of over $100,000.

I honestly believe that he did want me as a client he could "grow with." As a new financial consultant, he was starting a small business, after all. And all new entrepreneurs are delighted to obtain a little bit of cash flow today combined with the promise of future sales tomorrow. But no one in securities school or wherever he went to learn about financial consulting had taught him anything about the investments appropriate for somebody like me. A newly minted financial consultant may want to work with people like me, but the sophisticates who prepare the textbooks prefer to concentrate on the people who have enough cash to generate some *real* commissions. My "financial adviser" didn't fail me because he didn't care about me. He failed me because there simply *aren't* many securities products appropriate for someone like me, and those that exist aren't sold primarily through individual salesmen.

The Advantages of Partnerships

Nonetheless, I learned something from the projects he promoted and from other projects I've seen wealthy people put together.

First, some of the deals my financial adviser offered were in genuinely attractive fields, such as real estate. You could make money there, and you didn't need a multimillion-dollar venture capital pool to do it. But *you'd need to put together more money than I or most people under thirty-five have available.* There are not many good investments for a simple $5,000, but there are many good investments for $100,000 to $500,000, and you can safely leverage your way into them if you can scrape together $10,000 to $100,000 cash.

Second, many wealthy investors who could afford everything I couldn't afford actually *prefer* not to go into deals alone. In order to share risks, bring other people's skills into a project, and make sure someone else thinks an idea is as good as they think it is, they will join with other investors to form a partnership.

If people who can afford to get into deals on their own think it's a good idea to form partnerships, it's an even better idea for you and me, who probably couldn't get into the best investments by ourselves anyway. Partnerships with other creative, honest young people are likely to be the best investments you can find (except perhaps your own home).

Too many people think they have to wait to be rich before they can join partnerships. That may have made sense thirty years ago, when most partnerships were created among club members in old towns. Perhaps then you had to earn your way into the club before you could intelligently join a partnership. But we're part of the first mass-market generation in history. If you grew up with *Leave It to Beaver, Bullwinkle,* and Mars candy bars, went to college to the beat of rock 'n' roll and an assortment of hippie and post-hippie political ideas, and now are trying to pull all this together into some kind of sensible, useful life, then you have as much in common with others of your generation as the men of the downtown clubs had with other club members in the past. Lots of people in our generation have good business ideas; others have the related talents — financial know-how, communications savvy, marketing skill, or whatever. Many even have jobs that generate capital they're looking to invest. All these ingredients should be put together in useful projects.

The only expertise most people of our generation lack is the knowledge of how to structure and run a partnership, and those aren't particularly difficult tasks.

The Legalities of Partnerships

Essentially, there are three ways of structuring the kinds of partnerships I'm talking about, plus variations:

1. *A general partnership* You get together with partners and agree on how you will share the costs, risks, and benefits of a project. Legally, each partner is totally liable for anything that goes wrong, all profits are immediately taxable, and all losses are immediately deductible on your income tax return.

2. *A limited partnership* One or more general partners runs the business in return for a bigger share of profits and unlimited liability for any losses. *Limited partners* put up cash, but they don't participate in day-to-day management, and their liability is limited to a specified amount — usually the amount invested, but possibly more if a higher limit is specified in the partnership agreement. (Specifying a higher limit may enable the enterprise to borrow more from a bank and give the limited partner greater tax benefits.) Most commonly, the limited partner is the more well-to-do participant, while the general partner is the true entrepreneur. Profits and losses from the business are immediately taxable or deductible for both general and limited partners.

3. *A corporation/Subchapter S corporation* While a partnership is legally just an agreement between two or more people to

divide up the cost, work, losses, and profits of getting something done, a corporation is a well-defined and potentially immortal legal entity owned by stockholders.

When a corporation is founded, generally an entrepreneur or entrepreneurs set it up, put some money in, and issue themselves a good deal of stock — say, one share for every 10 cents invested. Then the corporation can sell stock at higher prices to other participants, or it can give stock or stock options at lower prices to employees as compensation for their work. The entrepreneurs will usually be employees as well, and will take a salary for their efforts. Then if there are profits, they can be paid to the shareholders in proportion to the number of shares held.

A corporation has three main advantages for a small enterprise:

- It is well-defined and thus can be relatively easy to set up, explain to people, manage, and ultimately sell to someone else if the shareholders decide they want to get out.
- Owners of the corporation are not liable for damages beyond the value of their original investment unless the damages are their own personal fault. (If you were a general partner in an enterprise and a visiting salesman slipped and broke his leg on the steps of your building, theoretically he could sue you for every cent you owned. If you simply owned stock in a corporation that owned the building where the accident occurred, no one could take your money — he could only take the corporation's money. However, if you were directly responsible for the corporation's misdeeds — say, in addition to being a stockholder, you were the manager of the building and you should have roped off the steps — you could be sued as an individual for every cent, even if your business was a corporation.)
- Owners of a corporation gain several valuable tax benefits. They need not pay personal income taxes on profits until they're paid out in dividends. And when they sell their shares, the profits can be considered capital gains and eligible for lower capital-gains tax rates.

An enterprise that expects losses in the first year or two should be established as a *Subchapter S corporation*. "Sub S" corporations pass profits and losses directly to their stockholders' income tax returns. Later, when the corporation appears to be becoming profitable, it can be converted into a regular corporation. However, sometimes the IRS does not look favorably at converting from a Sub S as soon as profits are realized. Be sure to seek legal and accounting advice before making this move.

The potential disadvantage of a corporation is exactly the converse of its first advantage: because a corporation's rules are clearly defined in law, it's not quite as flexible as a partnership. And the tax benefits of incorporating may be reduced if the corporation is liable for corporate income tax payments. Also, corporations are slightly more complex to establish legally than partnerships: they must be registered with your state secretary of state or attorney general. (But don't forget that partnerships also produce complexities for you. Any partnership that produces revenues must file a special partnership income tax schedule with the federal government.)

Any of these forms of business can go by almost any name you'd like. Tomorrow you could be doing business as "Worldwide Computer Co.," unless the name has already been taken by someone else. The only real restriction is that you can't call something "Inc." or "Ltd." or "Corp." unless it's a corporation. But to use "Company" or "Co." or most other business names, you don't even need to set up a partnership. All you have to do is register the name with your state government. Your town clerk should have the appropriate forms, and it will probably cost about $10. If you set up a business without a partner and without setting up a corporation, it's called a *proprietorship,* and you are a *proprietor.*

Choosing the Right Form

The different kinds of business structures are appropriate for different kinds of businesses.

Bruce Rueppel, whom I discussed in chapter 1, has a general partnership with an old college friend, Alex Blodgett, to buy and manage properties in Dallas. They've agreed to share duties equally and profits and losses equally. There's no reason for them to create a corporation. They both understand how they want to work together, and their management of the properties would make them legally liable to lawsuits even if they did incorporate. They don't need to shelter profits in the corporation because real estate, for reasons I'll explain in the next chapter, generates losses on your tax return even when it's making money for you.

But legally, their partnership doesn't own the buildings they've bought together. Bruce and his partner do some of their borrowing from the bank in the name of the partnership, but they own their building and take out their mortgages as "tenants in common." Banks usually insist on a form like this (though it has different names in other states) because it means both partners are completely liable for the entire amount of the loan. Bruce and his partner could jointly own the property but manage it through their partnership, but if they did, they'd have to file a separate partnership income tax schedule. By simply working together as "tenants in common," they can split all income and tax deductions equally and report them directly on their own individual tax returns.

Bruce and his partner will bring in other investors to put up some of the cash for their transactions, and as they do, they may set up limited partnerships that give them a big return for managing the properties and also shelter the partners who contribute the money from any possible liability if things go wrong.

On the other hand, Steve Gottlieb, who has set up a company to sell records of old TV theme songs (can you still hum the intro to *The Jetsons?*) used a Subchapter S corporation. His bankers preferred the well-defined form of the corporation.

And Matthew Reich, who set up Old New York Beer Company after learning to make beer on his kitchen stove, had his lawyers set up a complex deal. He owns a corporation that is the general partner in a limited partnership. His investors are the limited partners.

This deal has a variety of advantages. *Everyone* winds up with limited liability, just as if the business were a corporation. But the complex form allows a complex split of profits and losses. The limited partners get 99 percent of any losses — which will benefit them as tax deductions — while Reich gets 1 percent; then the partners get 90 percent of the profits until they've received three times their initial investment back, then they get 50 percent of the profits and Reich gets 50 percent of the profits. Drawing up the complex set of legal documents needed to set up a corporation like this could cost significantly more than setting up an ordinary business, but Reich followed the common practice of persuading his lawyers to accept work on a contingency basis: they would get paid when the deal got financed.

Organizing Your Partnership

The general rule in creating a partnership is this: pick people you know you can trust, and who are as much like you as possible. The more partners have in common, the less trouble there's likely to be. But also, pick people who complement your skills. A substantial business operation typically needs an idea person, a person who's good at managing things, and at least one person who's good at selling, for instance. The people who organized the 13–30 Corp. at the University of Tennessee and eventually took over *Esquire* had a person in each of these slots, and also one person who was particularly sober and who became the controller.

You should spend plenty of time talking through every issue you can think of related to the business. Discuss, for example, how long the partnership must last and what will happen if one of the partners gets transferred to the new Citibank branch in Bangladesh.

Occasionally there are good reasons for including people quite different from yourself in a partnership. Sometimes older, experienced businessmen seek younger partners to run new projects. You may get the older man's experience and the opportunity to run your own show with little personal investment. Sometimes, too, people who've made a fortune in business then sold their companies (or otherwise found some time on their hands) want to help younger entrepreneurs and invest some capital in their projects.

If you run across opportunities with people like this, take advantage of them. Most established, successful businessmen are glad to hear of new, interesting deals. And talking to them may be worthwhile. But even the most active investors join in only a small portion of the deals they discuss. You can find most kinds of expertise — and the money to get most worthwhile businesses started — from people under thirty-five. And there are people under thirty-five with almost every kind of experience you could need.

Drawing Up the Partnership Agreement

There are no firm rules about drawing up a partnership agreement. While few partnerships function perfectly for years without any written agreement at all, they are the exception to the rule. Misunderstandings occur regularly among partners, so write down what you've agreed on, including:

- what the business will do,
- who will do what,
- how the profits will be divided, and
- how the losses will be allocated.

Even if the business is a corporation, which means it will have a fairly standard set of incorporation documents prepared by a lawyer, the key participants should probably write down these points on a separate sheet of paper.

A sample partnership agreement appears in Appendix A. When you think you're nearly ready to write up a partnership agreement, look at the following list of issues. Have you discussed and agreed on each one? Should you say something about each of them in the partnership agreement?

1. What is the business of your partnership? (Your description should be concise enough to fit on the back of a business card; see chapter 8.) How far from the original plan are you willing to let the business stray? (After briefly stating your planned business, you may want to add, "and whatever other businesses the partners may mutually agree on.")
2. What are your objectives? Where do you want to be in two years?
3. What will be the business's name? How will day-to-day management be conducted? Who will do what, and when? Who has the power to make what decisions? Where will the offices be, and who will keep the books?
4. What will you do if the business needs more investment money (say, the building you bought as a partnership needs repair)?
5. Under what circumstances will you take other people into the partnership? How will they be treated?
6. What happens if someone wants to (or is forced to) quit? Will the other partners buy him out? Can he sell his share to someone

other than the partners if he is offered a higher price? If he must sell to the other partners, how will the price be determined?
7. How will disputes be resolved? (Agree on a mediator or on how a mediator will be chosen.)
8. Should spouses or other relatives of the partners sign a statement saying they accept the agreement?

Once you've drafted a partnership agreement — and perhaps when it's in the form of a very rough draft — you should show it to a lawyer. On small deals (you're joining with a friend to own a building, or a friend has offered to sell something you make) you shouldn't have to pay more than $100 or $200 to have a lawyer look over the agreement you've written. In a larger, more complex deal, the lawyer may get 2 to 5 percent of the money raised, though often he's paid with a piece of the deal rather than cash.

In any kind of deal, a good lawyer may be able to point out several issues you haven't thought of, but make the lawyer explain to you *exactly* why his suggestions are good. Uncomprehended legalese will just make your contract less useful. A partnership agreement should be written in plain English and clearly indicate how everyone is expected to act in every likely eventuality, thus making lawsuits among the partners nearly impossible. If legal gobbledygook interferes with that objective, don't tolerate it. (See chapter 9 for suggestions on how to choose a lawyer and decide when he's being useful to you.)

Keeping Friends Friendly

Often the biggest danger is not that the business will fail — most people can analyze the risks of a business and avoid investing money they can't afford to lose — but that the business will fail in ways that destroy friendships. Thus the most important task at the early stages is discussing all possible events, even the event you would probably prefer to avoid discussing: what happens if things don't work out? Not all ventures are going to succeed, and you and your partners must consider this possibility. Articulate the benefits, perks, and lifestyle that you are giving up to pursue this opportunity.

Another important task at the middle stages is keeping everyone — including the Internal Revenue Service — informed. Remember that if one partner cheats on taxes, the IRS will hound everybody. In addition, agree that everyone will know what's going on inside the company at all times, and especially when things are going badly. You should also agree on how you will buy out a partner who disagrees with the way your business is being managed. If you do all this, friendships may survive even if everyone loses every penny he put in.

Buying Living Space to Build Your Financial Health

Everybody needs a place to live. That — even more than the fact that "God's not making any more land" — indicates why real estate is the single most important investment opportunity for most people. You and millions of others need good homes, and you can make amazing profits by owning and managing real estate and thus providing the homes we all need.

Thus you should:

1. Invest right away in something you need anyway — a home of your own.
2. Consider more real estate investments, planning them so that they'll benefit you regardless of tax changes that may occur.
3. Do most of your real estate investing with other people's money. Banks know that real estate prices rarely fall, so they'll loan you 75 to 90 percent of the value of a property. There will be ways to keep most of your interest payments tax-deductible under almost any tax reform that's likely to be passed. And mortgage loans are generally "non-recourse" loans, which means that if worse comes to worst and you can't make the payments, the bank can take the house but can't then demand any more money from you.
4. Look first at real estate if you're looking for a truly big profit. People make big profits when they leverage their investments with other people's money and use knowledge that they alone possess. Borrowing to finance stocks and most investments other than real estate is risky, and tens of thousands of people know

all about every publicly traded stock you could buy. But not only can you safely borrow to buy real estate, you already possess unique knowledge of several neighborhoods and dozens of buildings. Only a few competing investors know them at all, and you can profit from your information by recognizing which buildings and areas deserve higher prices. You can get personal knowledge on other buildings and areas just by walking around and visiting them. You can come out of a real estate investment with a substantial pile of cash far more easily than from any other kind of investment.

Real estate also brings significant tax benefits. If you own a $100,000 building and the income from rents just covers your mortgage payments, taxes, and expenses, you may think the building is just breaking even. But from the IRS's point of view, you're suffering a big loss — and you'll still be able to report a substantial loss even under the most restrictive tax-reform laws anyone has proposed. You will file a "Supplemental Income" schedule with your income tax return showing a loss that could be as high as $7,000 because of depreciation. You can then subtract that amount directly from your taxable income. If your total tax bracket is 40 percent, your "breaking even" building could produce the equivalent of $200 to $300 per month in tax reductions — and thus extra spendable income.

This includes only interest and depreciation tax benefits that would remain available under all the tax plans recently under consideration at the federal level. Real estate would remain a fine investment under every one of them — as long as you shop carefully. (The tax law as this is written allows even more deductions. When calculating the after-tax cash flow of properties, don't count tax benefits that are under attack in Congress. Make sure that properties you're considering will continue to provide good value under all likely tax changes.)

Real estate should be most people's first major investment and it can be some people's only major investment. Thousands of moderately successful artists, actors, politicians, and others in erratic but worthwhile fields have supported their careers with a bit of intelligent real estate investing. It's no coincidence that people use architectural metaphors — "foundation," "keystone," "cornerstone," "pillar" — when they want to describe something that supports everything else. Buy real estate intelligently and it will support whatever you want to do in life.

Find Value in What You Know

Jim is among the top young professionals on Wall Street. He'll take home $200,000 in salary and bonus this year. Clients think he understands the markets better than anyone else they can find. So where does he invest his own spare cash? In housing renovations in the rundown old Philadelphia neighborhood where he grew up.

Of course, he loves the old brownstones. But he's not investing for love — he's investing because he knows others will share his love and will want the homes. Eventually they'll recognize the excellent values they offer and will pay handsomely for them.

Jim's following the fundamental principle *Invest in what you know*. Supply and demand determine prices for investments even more than for ordinary goods and services. The price today indicates the demand today, but if you can guess which investments will be more in demand next year, you will have guessed which ones will be worth more next year.

You can guess best when you stick with what you genuinely understand. The neighborhood where Jim is investing is considered "lousy" today, he says. But Jim knows from twenty-eight years' experience that it is stable even in its worst parts and likely to improve dramatically as students move in from the nearby University of Pennsylvania. Moreover, he has known the developer who's managing the project since he was two years old. The guy lives in the neighborhood and "he's a world-class weightlifter," according to Jim. Jim knows the neighborhood kids will think twice before trashing any of his properties.

Before you look at real estate in fashionable neighborhoods or at any exotic investments, be sure to look at housing in the neighborhoods where you live and where you went to school and where you grew up. (Often students are the first to discover the excellent housing values in neighborhoods that are just starting to improve.)

Buy Properties You Can Turn Around

Jim is also following another important principle: he's buying properties that sell for less than they are worth because they need improvements. Many first-time property buyers seek clean, newly remodeled places. But if you buy a finished house or apartment, you can't expect much profit. You'll be bidding against other buyers who are looking for exactly the same kind of place. And you'll pay a premium that will subsidize the contractor and the guy who sold it to you, who will have done exactly what you should: they bought a property that needed some fixing up and did the work after calculating how they could spend the least to increase the selling price most.

Don't buy anything you couldn't turn around in a month or two at a profit by adding a coat of paint. As you shop around, notice the difference between the selling prices of slightly dilapidated — but structurally sound — buildings, and of similar places with fresh paint, flower gardens, and other cosmetic amenities. "The idea is to find a property with the right things wrong with it," says Bruce Rueppel in Texas. Peeling paint, overgrown flower beds, and run-down interior furnishings are signs of a property you'll want to bid on. But avoid properties with more fundamental problems: wood rot, termites, leaky plumbing, flooding basements, or defective boilers. Some of these problems can cost tens of thousands of dollars to fix and consume an enormous amount of your time.

As a general rule, don't buy anything unless it's selling for at least 20 percent below what you think it's worth.

Know Your Strategy for a Particular Neighborhood

Different neighborhoods progress differently. New York City is a "quick flip" area — prices often rise rapidly when a neighborhood is improving. Thousands of people have turned $18,000 down into $100,000 or more this way. But in other markets you'll have to be more patient. The demand for housing in one-industry towns, for example, might fluctuate with the economic health of that industry. In Tulsa, Oklahoma, you'd better plan on holding until the oil market improves. Probably you can turn $5,000 into $100,000 in the Tulsa market, but you must base your investment on both the inherent value of the real estate and the likely future prosperity of the community.

Develop a strategy for your neighborhood, and be sure you understand it clearly. Evaluate what kind of home will most attract the people who will want to buy or rent in your area in a few years, and estimate how long you'll have to hold on to earn your profit.

If you're buying rental property, its value will rise as rents rise. There's probably a rule of thumb that relates rent rolls to prices in your area. (The rent roll is the amount of rent the building takes in in one year.) Bruce Rueppel notes that in many markets, eight times the rent roll is common where tenants pay utilities; if the landlord pays utilities, the value will of course be much less — perhaps five times the rent roll. Thus one way to project the value increases you'll create will be to project how much you'll be able to increase the rent the property commands. Using the formula that says buildings sell for eight times the annual rent roll, a $1-a-month rent increase (which increases the annual rent roll by $12) will increase a building's value by nearly $100.

By knowing your strategy, you can recognize the risks you're taking and tell more easily if you've miscalculated. New York's "quick flip" real estate market can be dangerous: sometimes the market gets overbought, a recession depresses prices, and people must wait several years to get out with what they paid. By understanding the market, you may be able to recognize warning signs and sell out before a crash. Tulsa has less downside risk if you buy carefully, but finding a buyer who'll pay the current market price may take longer.

Neighborhoods become good investments when they are just starting to improve. Find a neighborhood where prices remain reasonable but home and apartment owners are already painting and fixing places up, or where a big developer is making major renovations. Neighborhoods may also improve when a large commercial development is completed, especially if it brings in a few hundred new employees who would like to live near their jobs.

Don't pioneer in an area that seems likely to remain a slum. Wait for the big developers who have more to gain (and lose) to come into the neighborhood and pave the way for your smaller investment. A single small-scale renovator can't make a slum improve, and your property may never rise enough in value to justify your investment.

Get All the Information You Can on a Neighborhood

When you've picked a neighborhood or two, take time to get to know it. Visit numerous real estate agents and try to develop independent sources of information on what's for sale. A first-time buyer may have to buy through a broker, and he shouldn't begrudge the broker his fee: the broker generally earns it by simplifying the transaction. But remember, especially in purchasing multifamily buildings, that if a building is an exceptionally good deal, the broker will probably buy it himself. You may want to seek buildings that brokers don't yet know about.

One tactic is to visit buildings with brokers and ask the owners whether they know of other buildings for sale. Or you can simply walk around a neighborhood, knocking on doors and talking with people in the street. And virtually all cities have an apartment house association or landlords' council of some sort that represents landlords' interests and keeps track of information that property owners need. In smaller towns, the Chamber of Commerce may perform the same functions. In either case, you should try to visit the organization. The apartment house association can discuss problems of landlords in the community and areas where renovations are going on. It may even know of property owners anxious to sell. It's usually a good organization to join if you do buy property, as its staff may be able to help you find craftsmen or other help when you need it and guide you if you have a tax dispute with the local government. (On the other hand, many mediocre apartment house associations can't tell you much more than where to file building-permit applications in City Hall.)

Find the Motivated Seller

Real estate brokers will tell you that you need to move quickly on properties. Don't listen. There are plenty more around.

The real estate cliché is that you want to find the "motivated seller" — ideally a businessman who has been transferred to another city, needs to sell quickly, and doesn't want to deal with real estate people. The motivated seller is exactly what you're looking for. You can contribute more and make more money when you find someone who needs you, and the motivated seller definitely needs you. The motivated seller can also be an heir selling a property he inherited, or simply someone who has acquired too much property and can't meet the payments.

Make low offers on several properties. Don't be afraid to offer so little that the seller feels insulted. Soothe his feelings by explaining that you'll have a hard time affording the negative cash flow the building will produce even if he sells it to you at your offering price. You should probably never increase your offer out of sympathy for the seller. Make a low but fair offer and stick by it. And if an engineer's inspection turns up problems in any house you're considering, don't fear to ask for a further reduction in price.

Start by Buying Your Own Place

Mark is a twenty-four-year-old, modestly successful actor in Los Angeles. Like most young actors, Mark can't work full-time at his profession. He could be working as a waiter when he's not on a movie set, making perhaps $1,500 a month.

But Mark hasn't managed his life the way most young actors do. A few years ago, when he was a junior at Wesleyan University, he joined with two friends to buy a home. Each contributed $4,000 (Mark had saved the money from summer and part-time jobs). They bought a house for $57,000 and lived in it for a school year. They had agreed to divide up the responsibilities: one spent several weeks before school choosing and buying the house before school began. Another took responsibility for fixing it up, and the third took responsibility for general maintenance. (They spelled all this out in formal partnership agreements prepared by Mark's father, a lawyer.)

"The first process of buying a house was very painful," says Mark. "We misbudgeted terribly. We forgot to think about certain problems with repairs. In the first year, for example, heating costs were ridiculous." Yet after everything was added up, costs weren't much more than college room charges would have been. And the house sold at the end of the school year for $70,000. Mark pocketed a profit of about $3,000.

Mark and one of the other partners, a girl named Molly, bought another building to live in for their senior year, renting out rooms to other students. Then they sold it at a profit.

The money allowed Mark to spend a year in Europe and have some cash left over. He used it to join with a partner back in the Los Angeles area. They looked at 150 places before buying a house in Santa Monica for $120,000 with $15,000 down. A bank, recognizing the property's underlying value, agreed to grant a substantial loan that would cover much of the cost of repairs. "I was going to wallpaper a bathroom with my notes describing the houses I had seen," Mark says. Mark and his partner spent $25,000 fixing the property up and paying off some back taxes. They put in some grass, repainted, and knocked out a wall to create a larger master bedroom. The neighborhood was hot. When they were done, people began coming up to the door asking if they could buy the place. They sold it for $250,000.

Real estate supports Mark's career as an actor — though real estate is doing so well that Mark finds he must constantly remind himself that acting is his primary job. Because Mark started his investing career early, he can remain an actor and doesn't have to starve.

Making Sure You've Got a Good Deal on Your First House

A basic test of value in a home is: Could you rent it out for enough to cover your mortgage payments and taxes, with a little bit left over for some of your expenses? If not, there's something wrong with the deal. (A place won't necessarily rent for enough to cover *all* your expenses, however, and rent certainly wouldn't cover payments on personal loans or credit card debt taken on to buy it. A house should rent for a little bit more than enough to cover real estate taxes and the payments on a 90 percent mortgage. When you take account of the tax benefits of home ownership, you'll probably come out ahead even in the short-term.)

Occasionally all houses in an area will rise so much in price that nothing can be bought for a price that will meet this test. At those times it's usually a good idea to avoid buying in those areas. Prices may not rise much further anytime soon, and there's a significant risk that they will fall. If you must live in that area, rent a place for a while till you find a bargain.

The other important test of a good deal is a *thorough* report on the property from a qualified building inspector. Even the broker who's arranging the sale will urge you to have an engineer inspect it. (Telling you to get an inspection may reduce his liability to you: how can you complain that he hid the leaky roof when he specifically said you should have the building inspected before buying?)

Probably dozens of people operate as building inspectors in your area. If you don't know how to choose one, ask someone who has recently bought property for a recommendation. Don't rely on the broker's recommendation. After all, if the inspector tells you something is wrong, it can only create problems for the broker.

Most inspectors, who charge $120 and up for evaluating a property, are honest people who try to find a house's flaws and tell you about them. If you have a difficulty, it's likely to be communicating with the inspector, especially if you don't go with him when he looks at the property. Many building inspectors are experienced construction people. They're not noted for writing clear reports.

Be sure to go with your inspector. Ask lots of questions, and look in corners that he fails to notice. And put more faith in the inspector's comments than in vague assurances from an agent or a seller.

Alternatives to Buying Your Own Home

If for some reason you don't want to buy your own place, there are other ways of getting into real estate and doing just as well.

For example, several years ago Joe graduated from college and went to work for a bank — for the depressing salary of $15,000 a year. One of the perks, however, was that he could borrow $5,000 at modest interest whenever he wanted.

A friend in Boston wanted to buy a burned-out brownstone, renovate it, and flip it. They bought it together and turned it around in four months at a $4,000 profit. In the next three years they did similar deals on twenty more buildings and made $225,000.

If you don't want to buy a home — or if you feel you can't afford to — you're probably like one of these two people: either you can find a source of a *little* bit of capital, or your life situation will allow you to put in some sweat equity to improve a place. Look for a partner and invest with him or her.

Or you can look for any of dozens of special deals that always exist in real estate. Ask real estate brokers in your area if you can get a *shared appreciation mortgage.* Under this arrangement, a financier (often the seller) of a property puts up all the cash for the down payment on a property and a buyer who has no cash promises to handle all varying costs and maintenance. They form a partnership and buy the property; the person who had no cash at the time of the purchase can later buy clear title to the property for an amount equal to the down payment the financier originally put down plus half the price appreciation that has occurred since then. Both partners enjoy tax advantages, and you can come out way ahead by playing either the role of the financier or the role of the cashless buyer.

More exotic deals always exist. Marci, an administrator for the New York State government in Albany, got in on a Historic Rehabilitation Investment Tax Credit that let her take $7,000 more than her down payment *out* of the property when she bought it.

The Historic Rehabilitation Investment Tax Credit is a government scheme that helps rebuild many old structures in cities. If a historic building needs rehabilitation, the government will allow a tax credit for 25 percent of the certified rehabilitation cost. The catch is that owner-occupied housing isn't eligible, and the owner has to hang on to the property for five years.

A developer in Albany rehabilitated an old factory and sold the apartments as $72,500 condominiums that investors could rent out. The builder arranged financing for 90 percent of the condominiums' cost. Thus Marci bought the condominium with $7,250 down. But as the person who put the condo into service (i.e., first rented it out to someone), she was the person eligible for the tax credit. The rehabilitation cost amounted to 80 percent of her purchase price, so the tax credit was worth $14,500. She could apply that amount to her next year's federal tax liability or to recovering part of her last three years' tax payments. Thus she was immediately $7,000 ahead.

If the neighborhood does rather badly — and her property rises in value by only 3 percent a year — Marci will wind up with an enormous profit over the five years she must hold the property.

The Historic Rehabilitation Investment Tax Credit now seems likely to be abolished in the current wave of tax reform, but other similar opportunities frequently appear. Keep in touch with real estate professionals in your area and watch your local newspapers' real estate pages for such opportunities.

One other option is to invest with a friend who's already successful. For example, I know a banker and a real estate professional who met as students in California. Today they own six buildings jointly. They're each worth $250,000 on paper but have no cash, so they're organizing partnerships including old friends from school. The friends will each put $5,000 or more into purchases of a building. "Most of them are very successful, but they're only smart in their own fields," says my friend. "They're very bright engineers; they're very bright attorneys; they're very bright medical interns. They're making good money. But they've seen a lot of it disappear." Often someone who knows real estate can help get others started.

Finding the Right Loan

When you visit a banker, you're in an unusual situation. You're shopping; you're considering buying something and he's the seller, so you can benefit by taking an active, probing stance. At the same time, you're asking the banker to take a risk on you, so you must carefully assure him of your dependability.

It pays to start shopping for mortgage loans long before you make your first offer on a property. Try to know the personalities of the various banks in your area (see chapter 9).

Mortgage lending moves in cycles, and at some times loans come far easier and with better terms than at others. Watch newspaper articles about interest rates, particularly long-term rates. The best time to make offers is when rates have just come down. On one hand, many sellers will have been stuck with properties they couldn't get rid of because high rates in the recent past kept buyers from buying. On the other hand, newly lower rates will allow banks to give you a good deal.

Some bankers are flexible and hungry for mortgage business, especially when rates are low. Though the entire banking industry is in flux now (see chapter 9), it's still important to remember the distinction between *commercial banks,* which do all sorts of lending; *thrift institutions,* such as savings and loan associations, which traditionally specialized in home loans; and specialized *mortgage companies,* which exist exclusively to make mortgage loans and generally sell your debt to others. I can't predict which of these will offer the best deal in your area, but each will have its own personality. Institutions that plan to sell your loan to other investors will offer least flexibility. Others may be able to tailor a deal to your particular situation.

Banks offer many different kinds of loans today. The "conventional" loan — the fixed-rate loan for fifteen to thirty years — probably carries a higher interest rate than other mortgages. It should: dozens of small financial institutions have gotten in deep trouble over the past decade because they held too many low-interest, long-term mortgages when interest rates rose. Banks must cover themselves by demanding higher interest rates on these loans.

Don't be afraid of adjustable-rate debt. Payments on an adjustable-rate mortgage *may* rise substantially over time. But you *know* your rent will rise if you don't buy a home. Just be sure an adjustable-rate mortgage includes a reasonable payment "cap" so your monthly payment can't suddenly jump from $400 a month to $800 a month.

In the long run you want to establish relationships with bankers who will trust you and give you good advice. It may be worthwhile to pay an extra quarter or half point in interest to work with a good banker.

Planning to Cover Your Costs on Income Property

Whenever you buy income property, you need to budget carefully. You'll probably be stretching your assets thin to make your first purchase or two, and most properties will be a drain on your cash flow for the first year or so that you own them.

Make up at least two rough budgets for every income property you're seriously considering:

- a fix-up budget, to indicate what you'll have to put into the property over the first year or two, and
- a cash-flow budget, estimating the income and outgo you'll face each month after your fix-up program is completed.

Your fix-up budget will obviously vary with the building. Allow a minimum of $1,000 for each apartment unit even if you see nothing that needs doing except painting. And add in several hundred dollars for purchase of the tools you'll need.

Your cash-flow budget should include these expense items:

- Taxes: local property taxes plus any other taxes that may apply in your area.
- Utilities: water, sewer, garbage, electricity, gas, oil. Try to get a look at the owner's bills for the past couple of years. And be sure to learn whether the owner or the tenant pays each utility. A $350-a-month rent is quite a bit less if you must pay utilities than if the tenant must pay.

- General maintenance and supplies. One rule of thumb says that for a lower-middle-income multi-family building in good condition you should allow at least $100 a month for the building plus $50 per unit.
- Turnover expenses. Every time an apartment becomes vacant you must clean and probably paint it. Be sure to budget for this in advance.
- Payroll. You may want to give one tenant in an apartment building a discount on his rent in return for some work, especially if the building has more than a half a dozen units. If a building has more than fifteen units, you're likely to find you need someone full-time.
- Grounds maintenance. Paying someone to take care of the shrubbery can make a building much more rentable.
- Administrative costs. This includes signs or advertising to attract new tenants, licenses that may be needed, legal and accounting costs. Be sure to budget something for legal costs, as you'll surely need to evict somebody someday.
- Insurance. Shop around for policies; prices vary a lot.

When estimating the income the property will produce, the big issue is when you'll be able to raise rents and how much. Real estate agents often claim you'll be able to raise rents as much as 40 percent without any renovations at all. Sometimes, in fact, a bit of minor fixing up will let you raise rents by more than 100 percent. But will the market really support the rents projected? And are you really willing to evict the tenants on the second floor who can't afford $400 a month? Don't forget that you'll find tenants more easily if you charge a bit below the maximum rent you can get.

Make an allowance for vacancies and delinquencies. This is a good time to think about the worst tenant you can imagine. In most states you can evict a tenant who refuses to pay rent within sixty days after you've put your lawyer on the case. How many months' rent do you think you could lose from the worst possible tenant? Assume in your budget that you'll have one such tenant every two years or so.

After you've calculated expenses and income, estimate the property's effect on your personal tax picture. (See chapter 10 to learn how to calculate your *total tax bracket*.) You'll want an accountant to do your tax returns when you own property even if you never had one before, so while you're looking at property, look for someone to advise you on how much tax you'll be able to save because of a particular deal. Don't forget that if you do a deal that reduces your tax liability, you can benefit immediately by either reducing the amount of withholding your employer takes out of your salary (ask the person who handles the paperwork in your company for a W-4 form, and take more exemptions — see chapter 3) or by filing an amended estimated tax return for the next quarter if you're self-employed.

Now subtract estimated operating expenses from your estimated income. You should be able to project a positive cash flow emerging within eighteen to twenty-four months after you've bought a property: rents rise, and mortgage payments don't. And you may find you can make a profit from the beginning when you've taken account of tax benefits.

Try to keep your offers well under the "standard" rent multiple in your area, and seek buildings that will produce a positive after-tax contribution to your cash flow as soon as you've completed basic repairs. Rent multiples vary from market to market, but more than that they vary from deal to deal. Some buildings cost less than others because they consume more fuel, require more maintenance, or are located in an area where tenants are hard to attract. Some buildings cost less because rent-control laws limit the income you can expect in the long run (occasionally making them completely unprofitable). On the other hand, some buildings deserve to cost more because their current tenants are paying significantly less than a market rent. This rent can be immediately increased after the sale is completed. Most important, some buildings cost more than others because the seller drives a tougher bargain.

Think About Your Ethical Position

A key question that summarizes all the ethical issues and other sources of discomfort you may face is: How much will you want to raise rents? You'll probably want to avoid deals where you must evict people to make a profit. But you do need to think about both

- your ethical position, and
- the extent that you're comfortable asking tenants for what you think you deserve.

You *can* find deals where you'll never have to raise rents or evict anyone. You can buy vacant buildings and fix them up. You can concentrate on buying dilapidated houses you'll live in, improve, and "flip." Or you can learn how to convert existing buildings to condominiums or cooperatives without evictions. But the only reason for limiting yourself this way is squeamishness, not morality. People need rental housing, and the only way anyone can provide it is to raise rents to keep pace with costs. Landlords must also evict tenants who refuse to pay rent or destroy property.

In any case, you'll make your real money not by raising the rents of existing tenants but by renting out at market rates apartments that become vacant, and then later by reselling the building at a higher price that rising market rates will justify.

All this doesn't eliminate ethical questions and confusion, but it may make the questions easier. You'll probably want to ask tenants for a rent increase when you buy a building so that the higher rent can help you with your cash flow. On the other hand, you'll probably allow longtime tenants who are taking good care of the building, especially those without much money, to pay less than market rents. You can do that and still make an excellent profit.

So think about how *you* think a property owner should manage his building, and create a strategy that will let you manage that way.

Plan for Profit

You probably won't make the profits some real estate entrepreneurs in the 1970s did. The 1970s were an inflationary decade, and simply owning hard assets guaranteed not just good but spectacular profits.

But real estate offers enough profit margin, enough opportunity for leverage, and enough chances for you to benefit from your own intelligence that you can make money — even though many things are *guaranteed* to go wrong if you own property for very long. In the next chapter I'll talk about how to manage your property once you've got it. There's a lot to learn.

Even with all the drawbacks, complications, and possible pitfalls, real estate investments can do more for you in the long run than any other large category of financial dealing. Don't be so lazy or preoccupied that you ignore them.

Managing Income Property: A Quickie Crash Course

Successful real estate people believe deeply in Murphy's Law: If anything bad can happen, it will.

Virtually everyone I've met in real estate tells of "disastrous" experiences. If you don't look carefully at a seller's fuel bills, it will turn out that he understated them by 50 percent. If you guess that it will cost $300 to fix leaky plumbing, the plumber's bill will turn out to be $1,200. If you fail to check a tenant's references, he'll turn out to be a drug dealer.

Yet the people who have suffered these disasters all wound up making money. Some had to work harder than they expected to turn around properties. But I've never met anyone who lost money in real estate if he focused on buying *value*. And many have found that with a bit of intelligent planning they could make money while working no harder than they had worked on taking care of apartments they rented.

Real estate is both challenging and rewarding because you're managing something *tangible*. You'll probably find you feel effects of what you do much more keenly in managing properties than in a regular job.

Your objectives are simple:

- to manage your housing well,
- to be reasonably compensated by your tenants (if you have tenants), and
- to be well compensated through the profits you make when you sell.

Keep those objectives firmly in mind, and you'll become rich by creating value.

Turning Your Cash Flow Around

After you've purchased a property, you are immediately likely to face two difficulties:

1. Your building probably creates a negative cash flow for you, at least on a pretax basis. In other words, you're spending more money every month than you're collecting in rents or than you would be spending to rent a similar place for yourself.
2. Because you were looking for a bargain, you probably bought a building with problems. You want to eliminate the problems as soon as possible.

You want to obtain a positive cash flow and make the building presentable quickly.

Obviously the fastest way to improve cash flow in a building with tenants is to raise rents. Whatever you've chosen as your approach to rent increases, it makes sense to begin applying it early. Tell tenants the first time you meet them how difficult the purchase was for you. Explain how much the building is costing you in cash flow.

You probably don't want to raise rents before you've made some improvements. A coat of paint in the hallway will tell your tenants that you're serious about giving them something for their money. But unless everyone in the building is already paying a full market rent, you should raise rents to some extent soon after buying. Your tenants can appreciate how much you need the money then.

From the time you take over a building, everything you do should be based on a strategy for making it profitable.

Vacant Apartments: An Opportunity

Your biggest gains will come when an apartment becomes vacant and you need not fear to set a substantially higher rent. Remember that in raising rents you're not only increasing cash flow, you're also increasing the value of the building, often by as much as $1,000 for every $10 of monthly rent increase.

You don't just want to fill the vacant apartments, you want to fill them with good tenants who will pay their rent on time and take good care of the building. The true market value of an apartment may vary by as much as 20 percent depending on which well-informed landlord is establishing it. Consult other real estate owners in your neighborhood before setting your rent. And remember that you'll get tenants more quickly if you ask for a rent at the lower end of the market value range.

Before you even set a rent, however, do some fixing up. You'll have to clean and paint. Carpeting, new bathroom fixtures, and a thorough cleaning of hardwood floors are also good investments. Hardware stores can sell you a special solvent for cleaning hardwood floors. It's usually more cost-effective than sanding them down. Hire someone to clean and paint if you don't enjoy doing those jobs yourself. Other real estate professionals in your area can recommend people who'll work for very reasonable prices.

Bruce Rueppel in Dallas usually installs ceiling fans for about $100. They're highly fashionable there and they let him charge an extra $10 a month or so. Other amenities are attractive in other markets.

As you're improving the apartment, think about how you'll seek a tenant. An expensive classified ad in a big newspaper may work no better than a notice posted on a bulletin board in the local Laundromat or some photocopied flyers. But you want to put your announcement in a location where the type of tenant you are seeking will see it. An "Apartment For Rent" sign on the building may be seen mainly by young toughs who hang out in the neighborhood with nothing to do. They aren't the kinds of tenants you want. If you hope to improve the quality of your neighborhood, you may want to advertise in a newspaper read by upwardly mobile people. But this won't do any good if your apartment is in an area where such people still don't want to live.

Be cautious in selecting tenants. Ask for references and telephone all of them. Don't believe hard-luck stories unless someone proves them to you. Kit Barry in Brattleboro, Vermont, found it was almost always a mistake to rent to someone under twenty years old. "There was an eighteen-year-old. The social welfare department brought him and he looked sad and innocent and they told me how he came from a broken family and everything. So I said, 'What the hell, give the kid a chance.' Then he moved in and all hell broke loose. He let his friends in and they just methodically set about wrecking the place."

The moral is that business will force you to face the evils of human nature, and you must protect yourself by requiring proof of people's responsibility.

Improving Your Property

Some professional real estate developers tell me that they try to create $200 of value for each $100 invested in a property. Since you'll be doing more of your installation and fix-up work yourself than a well-financed professional would, you'll probably want to raise your property's value by $300 or $400 for each $100 *spent*. That's an entirely realistic goal.

When you are improving a house you own, you should concentrate on improving the property in ways that will make it more valuable when it comes time to sell. If you have tenants, remember the rule that improvements that support higher rents increase the property's value substantially. Try evaluating improvements by thinking about how much they'll allow you to raise rents and how higher rents will affect property value.

Cosmetic improvements can increase a property's value enormously. I know one real estate man who typically buys buildings, paints the corridors and repairs broken fixtures, fixes up vacant apartments, and then either sells the building or converts it into a coop under a plan that involves no evictions. He seeks to triple his money in three years, and he usually succeeds.

The most important items in making a property valuable don't cost much. Take care of them quickly after you've bought a property, and see that they're taken care of efficiently for as long as you own it.

- Paint the exterior, corridors, and possibly other areas.
- Keep all fixtures working, including building security fixtures.
- Install hallway carpeting, if appropriate.
- Maintain and repair any woodwork.
- Maintain a small amount of "landscaping," such as a flower bed or box in front of the building.

Other items cost more and are more trouble, but you can't ignore them. A good how-to book, such as the *Reader's Digest Complete Do-It-Yourself Manual* (published by the Reader's Digest Association), is indispensable. So is a good set of tools. Don't skimp on these essentials.

Try to find one store where you can get everything you'll need. A large lumberyard/home-repair store is likely to be more helpful than a small hardware store, and since you'll be doing more business there than the average homeowner, you can get to know the staff. Learn which staff members are helpful and ask lots of questions. Also, find out which building-materials manufacturers maintain toll-free (800) numbers to advise do-it-yourselfers.

You don't need to do everything by yourself. Most real estate people can recommend inexpensive cleaners and painters. Cleaning may cost as little as $25 for an apartment; painting as little as $100. Put your do-it-yourself skills to work on plumbing and, if you know how to do it, electrical work. Plumbers and electricians can cost as much as four times what cleaners and painters charge.

Though zoning laws and building codes are a nuisance, be sure to follow them. When in doubt, see a lawyer about what's legal. Many property owners skimp on legal fees and try to do without permits they should obtain. But doing everything legally is worthwhile even if you must borrow to pay legal fees. You want to be sure you'll be able to benefit from your improvements later on, and if you've violated a building code, you never know when the building inspector will serve you with a summons.

The trick is to accomplish each repair quickly and efficiently. Even operating an eight-family building can be only slightly more complex than managing a single-family house. Whichever you own, you want to invest a few hours regularly and perhaps a few hundred dollars a month to create a building you'll sell at a profit.

Remember your goals. If you keep them in mind when managing your building, you'll do well.

When to Sell

Unless you fall in love with your property or you're trying to raise children there, you'll want to sell when its price appreciation peaks. In other words, you want to hold on while the price is rising rapidly, but then sell. This may seem like just another version of the old stock market advice, "Buy low, sell high." That's easy to recommend, but generally hard to do. In real estate, however, picking a good time to sell is easier than in the stock market. When you buy, you should have an idea of what your property will really be worth when properly cared for. You should guess how long it will take to achieve that price, but recognize that your guess may be wrong.

As soon as you've made the place presentable, it's time to start looking for the right time to sell. You have to hold for six months to qualify for long-term capital-gains tax treatment, but after that it generally makes sense to find out what the market will bear.

Evaluate whether your original price goal still makes sense. If it does, put your property on the market, asking a bit more than the price you feel it will ultimately be worth. If you can sell for roughly your long-term goal, you should probably conclude that the property has already achieved most of the price appreciation you can reasonably expect. Accept the offer and flip yourself into some other bargain asset.

If you can't get your target price, reevaluate the situation every six months or so. Does your target price still make sense? Can you get it if you sell now? Unless you've badly miscalculated, you'll soon find an opportunity to sell at a good profit.

Do You Need a Broker?

Almost any real estate brokerage firm will appraise your house for you at any time for free. They hope you'll decide to sell the house through them. Take advantage of these offers.

Some of the people mentioned in this book suggest that you may not even want to use a broker when you sell. Brokers typically charge commissions of 3 to 7 percent. When you buy a house through a broker, the price includes the commission. But when you sell, you pay the commission directly, and it can substantially reduce your profit. If you buy a property for $60,000 and sell it for $80,000 through a broker, paying a 6 percent commission, you'll pocket a profit of only $15,200.

But if, instead of hiring a broker, you advertise the house yourself, and pay several hundred dollars to a lawyer to handle the details of transferring the property, you might come out ahead. If you buy a house for $60,000 and sell it yourself for $80,000, you may spend $200 on classified ads and such and $800 or so on a lawyer to handle the details. You'll pocket a profit of $19,000.

That's an extra $3,800 for what could be as little as a few hours' work.

However, beware that this works only if you are a decent salesman. Brokers generally have access to more customers than you do and can also take care of the many details involved in the transaction.

Refinancing

If for any reason you don't want to sell your property right away, watch for an opportunity to profitably *refinance* it — that is, to borrow against the increased value of the property, preferably at a lower interest rate than you originally paid.

Sometimes refinancing is actually more profitable than flipping, because you avoid the costs of selling. Say you bought a property for $60,000 with an 80 percent ($48,000) mortgage. The value has risen to $80,000. A new 80 percent mortgage would amount to $64,000. That would allow you to pay off the original mortgage, pay $1,000 in refinancing costs, and keep $15,000. If you can choose a time when interest rates are 3 percent lower than when you took out your original loan, your new monthly payments won't even be higher than your old ones. (Refinancing is almost *never* profitable during high-interest-rate periods.)

You can also take a simple equity loan against your property to finance almost anything. You'll pay a higher interest rate than on a standard mortgage, but you can avoid the fees banks charge when an entire loan is refinanced.

The Rewards of Managing on Your Own

Many people think of real estate investing as requiring the skills of a gnome of Zurich. They're wrong.

Profiting in real estate mainly requires skills you've already got: the abilities to recognize a bargain and take care of a home. Just trust your common sense. It *will* bring you closer to your life goals.

Venture Capitalism on a Budget

Steve Gottlieb turned down a dozen friends (including me) who said they wanted to invest in his business.

"I figured, land one big investor and save myself a lot of paperwork and legal complications, not to mention hand-holding. With degrees from Yale College and Harvard Law, I knew I could get in the right doors. The rest would fall into place. After all, I had grown up in a marketing-driven family business, had some experience managing a company, and had a sexy idea that anyone who had ever heard the term 'baby-boomer' could understand. The idea: a record album of TV theme songs, from *Star Trek* to *Mister Ed, The Flintstones* to *Mission Impossible.* If the idea alone wasn't exciting enough, I had half a dozen ancillary products, from a Volume II to a TV merchandise mail-order catalogue. The whole business was going to be done through direct-response TV advertisements so the overhead would be almost nonexistent. Beyond this, I had a partner who was loaded. He was financing a good part of the venture, and with his name attached to the company, bank financing would be cake," Gottlieb says.

"What I found out, though, was that the people with lots of money also had lots of opportunities. And even though they might think my business plan was terrific, they passed up good deals every day of the week. They certainly felt no remorse in simply wishing me luck on my crapshoot, however sexy. I met lots of nice folks (they typically bought lunch), and thought perhaps these initial good impressions would pay off in the next go round — if this go round ever got going."

But getting it going was proving more and more difficult. On the day they were to secure a loan to get the company rolling, even Gottlieb's rich partner began to think of other opportunities. "Sometimes people who've grown up rich get uncomfortable about paying their way. My partner's unearned wealth made him paranoid about being valued for anything other than his nonmonetary, intangible contributions. I guess that's a good way of staying rich, but as he wasn't working in the business, his intangible contributions didn't justify much tangible return. I told him his money had to be on the table or I'd go it alone.

"What killed me was the eleventh-hour timing of his cold-feet attack. On the day we were supposed to close with the bank, I had just parted with my absolute last dollar. My most recent apartment sublet was about to expire and I had no idea where I'd be sleeping in a week. I had been unable to get a lease and had been moving my 'office' on almost a monthly basis. Meanwhile, the guy with the mega–trust fund was going to let the whole deal cave in if he didn't get a couple percentage points more than had previously been agreed to."

So Steve took my money. And he took other friends' money. He financed the whole business that way in four weeks. "I was really surprised how much opportunity there was with guys I considered just like me. These people had become investment bankers or lawyers, and they had gotten their bonuses after their first three years or whatever, and they were just dying to get into something a little bit more exciting than investment banking or law."

Steve had discovered something that many experienced businessmen know but that rarely gets into the media: some of the best "venture capital" investors are those with limited means. Any accountant will tell you that professional "venture capital firms" represent no more than a tiny fraction of the funds invested in small businesses. The rest comes from friends and relatives of entrepreneurs and from a few seasoned businessmen who recognize the potential of a few start-ups and invest in them as a sideline.

Entrepreneurs' friends — especially friends who've made a little bit of money doing things that the entrepreneur will need to understand to succeed — are in many ways the best possible investors. They have time and often expertise that richer investors lack. They can poke holes in your idea in a friendly way. And unlike many big-money investors, they haven't grown to expect that a business must guarantee them a million-dollar return on investment in five years to be worth bothering with.

At the same time, friends' businesses are often the best possible investment for young people with just a little bit of money — say $5,000 to $10,000 that they can afford to gamble with. In evaluating them and contributing to them, you use your special talents to add value. Just as you avoid competing with pension funds and other big investors when you buy and manage real estate, you contribute in unique ways when you invest in new businesses. The risks are *much* greater than the risks of investing in real estate. Most people should invest in real estate first and in business ventures only after they've built an equity cushion in their real estate against a rainy day. But you can structure the deals so the rewards in venture capitalism can ultimately be far greater than most investors achieve in real estate.

The young people who invested $5,000 and up in 13–30 Corp. when it was little more than an idea have received 40 times their original investment and more. A woman I know put $5,000 into Old New York Beer Company simply becuse she had some spare cash after selling a car. (She and her husband didn't need two cars in New York City after they got married.) She knew about the opportunity because she had taken a wine course from Matthew Reich, who was setting the company up. Old New York Beer Company has already doubled the worth of her investment after a year and a half, and she stands to increase it substantially if Old New York's New Amsterdam Amber Beer continues to sell well.

Searching for Opportunities

The simplest way to search for opportunities is to listen to plans of friends and relatives. "Putting out the word" that you're looking may be dangerous. Play a little bit hard to get, or you'll attract a lot of flaky ideas from people who don't want to give you much money even if they succeed. Everybody has a brother-in-law who'd like to borrow $10,000.

On the other hand, it's very reasonable to tell your accountant (or whoever does your income tax return), your lawyer, your banker, and any other financial professionals you know about your desires. Real entrepreneurs often mention their financial needs to these people. You can talk openly to people who know about how deals are really structured — but be much more cautious with anyone who's likely to think that a good investor simply lends money and maybe takes 12 percent a year interest.

Your Role

Steve Gottlieb asked an investor who's an investment banker for advice about structuring the deal, got legal advice from an investor who's a lawyer, and talked to me for advice about publicity and sales. Other entrepreneurs ask much less advice from investors. But you're probably better off choosing to work with an entrepreneur who asks you good questions. Here's why:

1. A business that needs your special expertise, whether in art or personnel management or sociology, is usually a better opportunity for you than one that doesn't because it gives you a chance to add more value. Thus you can ask for and expect to get more reward.
2. It's far easier to judge the shrewdness of a businessman and the progress of a business if he's asking you questions than if he thinks he doesn't have to. If you're involved in business planning, you're also likely to learn earlier when something is wrong.
3. Entrepreneurs who seek advice are generally better businessmen than entrepreneurs who don't. A willingness to look for advice is a sign that the person is driven by the market and not by ideas that will be hard to change if they turn out to be wrong.

Incidentally, the best way to test the truth of what you think you know is to use it in a real-life business situation. If you've studied psychology and you have nothing useful to tell an entrepreneur who will be managing people, then perhaps your training has left a few gaps regarding the real world.

Structuring the Deal

Steve structured his business as a Subchapter S corporation. He took 55 percent of the stock for his work; eleven investors who put in a total of $150,000 got 45 percent. In addition, he structured the deal so that one-third of the money we investors put in was loans, rather than equity. Thus we'll get back at least $50,000 plus interest before Steve can take out any profits on his 55 percent share.

Steve could borrow an additional $100,000 from the bank. (Our debt is *subordinated* to the bank's debt, which means the bank gets paid back before we do.) Steve now pays himself a salary from our (and the bank's) money. He's using the rest of the money to produce a double album of TV songs and a television commercial to promote it. The commercial has run on late-night TV in leading markets. (Have you seen a TV ad with a guy in the shower whistling the theme from the *Dick Van Dyke Show?* That's it.)

When Steve gets enough orders to pay his bills and his salary and leave some left over, the profits will be split 55–45 with us. The business plan says that will have happened by the end of 1985.

As a Subchapter S corporation, TeeVee Toons allows everyone to deduct any losses the company suffers from his or her tax return. On the other hand, if TeeVee Toons makes a fortune, we won't have much tax shelter until the business can be converted to a regular corporation, because Subchapter S corporation profits are directly taxable as ordinary income.

Because it is a corporation, the investors' liability is limited if anything goes wrong. If TeeVee Toons loses a lawsuit, the victors can take the money I put in but can't take any more from me.

Andy Gaspar, managing director of the large venture capital firm Warburg Pincus, warns that it's important to understand these legal details. "Know what, exactly, you are buying," he says. "I'm working on a situation now where I'm certain that a guy has sold 50 percent of his business to three separate individuals. This guy didn't do it intentionally but he got caught up in the heat of making promises. Even if someone is no crook, he can promise the same things to many people." When only the lawyer knows exactly what's in the legal documents that set up a business, everyone is likely to wind up unhappy.

Also, Gaspar notes, be sure to think realistically not only about the likelihood that you'll lose all your money, but also about the likelihood that your money will be tied up for a long time. A successful business needs an enormous amount of cash to keep expanding. Many can't pay their investors anything for as long as seven years.

The basic principles of all successful venture capital deals are usually the same, however. The entrepreneur should be making sacrifices — big sacrifices, if he's never done a successful deal before — to make his company succeed. He should get the chance to make big money if his business works. You, on the other hand, should stand to make a big profit on the money you've put in, but not as much as the entrepreneur.

Choosing a Deal

Generally, you shouldn't invest unless there is a possibility of a significant "upside" to justify your downside risk. Many people take big risks for too little potential return.

Chris Whittle, the chairman of 13–30 Corp., advises, if you are investing solely for financial reasons, that "unless an investment will significantly change your financial situation, don't do it." Perhaps that overstates the case a bit for people living on salaries. A good but very small venture capital investment is a chance to learn about entrepreneurship as well as to make good money. Moreover, you may have motivations that aren't financial in entering some deals: you may want to help renovate a neighborhood or get involved in a project that relates to your own special field.

But the point is this: don't invest unless you've got a chance for a really substantial profit in exchange for the substantial risks you're taking. If you put $1,000 into an investment that offers no more than the returns of an excellent stock market investment — say, the possibility of a 30 percent rise in value over a year — you're risking all your cash for a return that will probably be just about enough to buy a dinner for two after allowing for taxes and inflation. Why bother?

Whittle offers two excellent tests of a good investment: "First, *know the person you are investing in.* Make sure that this person feels a real obligation not to lose your money. There should be almost a guilt factor.

"Second, you should *see a chance to make 20 to 40 times your money.* If you have the possibility of losing all your money, you should see this chance. And in most speculative investments, you can lose all of your investment. It may take years to see that return. But you must make sure that the principals are committed to the long haul in order to see that gain. They must have a vision. The payout for 13–30 occurred between seven and fifteen years.

"If you can't satisfy these two criteria, keep your money in the bank."

Venture capitalist Andy Gaspar adds: "The key to the business is the individual. How committed is he to doing this business? What has he got to lose? There is a major difference between a dreamer and a doer. Some marketing guys have millions of good, in fact, great ideas. Will they stick to the one that you are funding?"

A venture capitalist in California told me that his firm had funded a guy who had a great idea for a new business. They put in the money and the guy was on his way. Three months later, the entrepreneur came in for a board meeting and made a presentation on a business that was not remotely related to the original proposal.

Many lawsuits and headaches later, the venture capitalist got his money out. Be sure you don't get into a similar situation. You won't have the legal clout to pull your money out, and you'll find the entrepreneur may never settle on anything. Your money is likely to be gone forever.

I'd add a few extra points to Whittle and Gaspar's suggestions:

1. Think about your entrepreneur/friend's experience and lifestyle, and whether you think he's suited to be a true entrepreneur. Many successful entrepreneurs are sons and daughters of entrepreneurs. A corporate bureaucrat may be an excellent person, but if he is accustomed to the care of a big organization, he may not anticipate events and react fast enough in the real world.
2. Is your friend the type who is going to admit his deficiencies and do something about them? Beware of arrogance. An arrogant entrepreneur is likely to fail until failure teaches him some humility.
3. Can your friend stick to one idea? Gene Murrow, a former math teacher who set up one of the first personal-computer stores in California, notes that in some respects an entrepreneur needs "tunnel vision." "You have to pick your niche and stick with it," he says. "A teacher is open to new ideas. Educating is asking many questions and understanding that there may be no right answers. In business, the same kind of thinking is called 'indecision,' and 'vascillation.' " The entrepreneur needs a peculiar combination of a flexible willingness to adapt to market changes and a stubbornness that keeps him from taking his mind off his single goal.

4. What does your friend know about the specific market he's entering? How much research has he done on that specific niche? Lots of people think there's a niche for a magazine to serve Catholic Mortuary Workers or some such group — and maybe there is. But before you invest in *Catholic Mortuary News,* you should see that the entrepreneur has solid facts to show that the market is strong.
5. How plausible are your entrepreneur/friend's answers to "What if . . .?" questions. Does he dismiss suggestions that catastrophes are likely to befall his business? If so, let him find another investor.
6. What is your own independent assessment of the risks the business faces? Even excellent entrepreneurs are almost useless in projecting risks. (The most successful often won't acknowledge that a course of action involves risk, even though they are making plans to deal with problems just in case.)
7. Marketing men say a good business needs a *unique selling proposition* — something it can offer buyers that no one else can do as well. Does your candidate have a unique selling proposition? How is it different from what other businesses are offering? Do you believe in its value?
8. Is the idea simple? As I'll discuss in the next chapter, simple ideas are the most likely to succeed.

Professionals often look at hundreds of deals for every one they join. You may not get the chance to be that picky, but you should plan on looking at five or ten ideas — at least — before you invest in anything. Remember, an entrepreneur is asking you to invest your money in a scheme that is supposed to make *him* wealthy. Make sure your chances of getting rich from the deal are good.

Invest in People

I used all of the above criteria in sizing up Steve Gottlieb and TeeVee Toons. Steve hit the market right on budget and only a couple of weeks behind his business plan. But from there everything went downhill — except, fortunately, Steve. His direct-response ads hit television stations around the country with an overwhelming silence. WTBS, a key outlet for his advertising, thought his commercials were silly and refused to run the spots. On the stations where he could run the ads, not enough people were calling in with orders to cover the cost of advertising. In short, the company was foundering.

At this point Steve could have cut his own losses and walked away from the business having lost only a year's labor, leaving the investors to take the losses. Worse still, he might have followed the business plan relentlessly and driven the business right into the ground, making the damage substantially worse for all involved. But he remained determined.

While determination and imagination are often not enough, in the case of TeeVee Toons they did the trick. A month after Steve had come to me with the unhappy prospects of refinancing, or liquidating, he had managed to turn the operation around. The disappointment he had faced in mail order had led him to experiment with a number of alternative distribution channels. Six weeks after the initial bad news, he had proven that the record could be sold at retail stores. Using his previous wholesaling experience, Steve set up his own distribution network going directly to stores. By this time he had broken even. A few short weeks later, he was turning down distribution advances from record companies that would have tripled our initial investment. The record pundits told Steve that the record had a good likelihood of going platinum (1 million copies sold).

A Small Start for a Good Business

A small-scale venture capitalist needs to understand both the possibilities and the dangers of investing. Take Michelle Marion, a 1980 graduate of the Cornell School of Hotel Management. As a junior hotel manager she had made good money for several years both in summer jobs and in a hotel-industry job after graduation. In 1982 she and a friend were looking for a place to invest.

A friend introduced them to Bill Haney, a nineteen-year-old Harvard student. Haney, the son of a Newport, Rhode Island, schoolteacher, had come to Harvard a year and a half earlier with $10 in his pocket. To pay for school he had worked "dorm crew," the lowliest of the low student jobs at Harvard — essentially a maid service using students as maids. He was desperate to make some money.

Haney turned out to be a born entrepreneur. "A guy showed up at my door selling firewood. I told him that I owned the franchise to sell firewood at Harvard, even though I didn't," Haney recalls. "We then decided to split the operation fifty-fifty. We made several thousand dollars in a couple of days." Haney and his friend became partners and set out to look for other business opportunities. "The difference between us and a lot of people who talk about starting businesses is that when we saw something that looked interesting, we pursued it," Haney says.

"About the thirtieth thing that we saw was a subway ad from an inventor who wanted a couple of guys to sell his product that injected platinum into car engines," Haney continues. "It would make the cars run better.

"We went to see the inventor and this guy was an absolute nut. He had a basement office in Brookline, Massachusetts. He was the whole company: R and D, sales, marketing, everything."

Haney found that the invention improved combustion on some cars and not on others. He and his friend scrounged together a little money, bought some of the gadgets, and then resold them. They met with the head of United Parcel Service and Ford Motors research. They then got the idea that this product could also work in oil-fired boilers.

They persuaded the father of a friend to invest $10,000 and obtained the exclusive rights to the use of the patent for boilers in the United States and Canada. They then set up a corporation, Fuel Technology, Inc.

They tested the product on boilers and the tests cut fuel use sharply, Haney says. Then they started to look for more money. A good friend of Bill's was sleeping on a friend's couch in Washington, D.C., and heard that Michelle Marion and her friend might be interested in investing some money. Michelle knew something about combustion technology and concluded that Haney's operation made sense. She and her friend put in $20,000 at 25 cents a share.

Haney invested some of Michelle's money in a trip to England, which led to a placement of $6 million in British venture capital. The price of shares rose in each successive financing. Michelle and her friend paid 25 cents a share. Now they own 10 percent of the company for $20,000, while the British investors put in $6 million. Other investors have put in an additional $25 million, which was mostly used to purchase eight small companies that could benefit from Fuel Technology's expertise.

Fuel Tech's first sales were in April of 1984. By April 1985, it had sold $10 million worth of combustion-related products. Haney projects $20 million in sales between April 1985 and April 1986. Recent investors in the company have paid $15 a share, which makes Haney's share worth $12 million on paper and Michelle and her friend's share worth $1.2 million.

But that doesn't mean that life has been perfect in Fuel Technology, or even that Michelle will ever see a penny of that $1.2 million in cash.

In 1983, Michelle left the hotel business and with two others opened a Washington, D.C., office for Fuel Technology. They were to sell its products to the federal government and others and take a commission. But they found that the products weren't yet sufficiently proven to fit on government procurement lists. The office was closed in less than a year. Michelle estimates that she earned only $10,000 or so each year between 1981 through 1984 — and she hardly lived the life of a budding millionaire. Today she has her own computer software business and can live well again. But she still doesn't know when she will get any direct benefits from her "$1.2 million" stake in Fuel Technology.

Despite the roller-coaster — or perhaps because she enjoys the roller-coaster better than she enjoyed hotel management — Michelle has no regrets. "If something else like Fuel Technology came along, I'd get in in a second," she comments. "I like a 'hands-on' investment. It's much better than just checking my newspaper every day to look at my stocks."

Big Risks, Big Rewards

If you have money to invest that you can afford to lose, look for good, low-budget venture capital opportunities. And if you have a business idea, be sure to consider your friends as possible investors.

The risks in any kind of venture capitalism are enormous, but you can easily wind up making yourself financially independent while helping create another 13–30 Corp. or Fuel Technology.

Creating Your Life's Business

Many people don't want to invest in other people's businesses: they'd prefer to become independent themselves. They may not think of themselves as entrepreneurs, but generally they'll do better if they learn to think of themselves that way, at least a little bit. Whether you want to establish a clinical psychology practice, become an independent artist, save the starving in Africa, become richer than the Rockefellers, or just live well without the hassle of full-time employment, you'll achieve your goals better if you think of them, at least to some extent, as the goals of a business. All these ways of life — as well as more ordinary businesses — demand that you meet three basic challenges:

- setting a clearly defined goal or goals,
- becoming good enough at your chosen task to justify the expenditure of someone's money, and
- motivating others to buy your product.

The three steps are obvious in ordinary businesses, especially in those that make a lot of money in a short time. But you'll find each of them is vital, whatever kind of life you're trying to establish.

Put Your Goal on the Back of a Business Card

Developing a clear idea is probably the most important step. There's a useful saying:

*If you can't write your idea clearly on the back
of a business card, you don't have a clear idea.*

The idea need not be profound. Brett Johnson set up Crowd
Caps in Minnesota after he picked up an inexpensive painter's cap
in a hardware store in 1980. His idea was simple: "I'll put team
logos and slogans on painters' hats and sell them at a reasonable
price to college students." He had built a $7.1 million business by
1983.

Once the idea is clear, developing a quality product is a straightforward challenge. Motivating people to buy it may not be easy,
but at least you'll know what you're selling and why people should
want it.

People who set up professional firms or try to establish some
other independent way of life usually see their planned way of
living as special. They often don't see the need for a clear idea or
for carefully motivating people to buy their product.

And in fact, they don't need as striking an idea as is needed for
a business that seeks big profits. A business that's going to produce
a forty-fold return on investors' money needs a "unique selling
proposition." A person creating a way-of-life business needs first
of all an *understandable* selling proposition. "It took me almost a
year to figure out how to explain what I wanted to do so that people
could understand it," says a San Francisco–based computer consultant. She now tells people, "I help people install computerized
systems in their companies in ways that cause their goals to be
met." Many other people do similar work, but her focus on the
businessman's goals, rather than a particular specialty, is just slightly
unusual. And she's willing to work with many different kinds of
software. Until she defined her business clearly, that willingness
sounded more like disorganization than like a benefit for potential
customers. The stating of her goal was a vital step toward creating
the business she wanted.

Starting Small

Whatever business you want to establish, you'll do best if you act
quickly on your idea and, if you have limited experience and training, start small. Most people who succeed as free-lance artists,

writers, or consultants begin free-lance work when they're still on someone else's payroll.

Even if you have a substantial bankroll or people willing to finance you, seek cash flow from your business from the start. If your idea is good, *somebody* should be willing to pay you for *something* related to it. I know a guy who decided in the mid-1970s that America needed a book on what it could learn from Japan. He dropped a successful free-lance writing and editing career in order to write the book, but he only collected rejection letters while other writers, starting later than he did, prepared books that became best-sellers. He now believes that he would have succeeded if he had defined his ideas concisely and used them as the basis for free-lance articles.

Meeting your goals will turn out to involve enormous amounts of petty detail that seems peripheral to your business. "If you can spend 20 percent of your time on the stuff that you want to do, you're doing good," says a former bureaucrat who founded a non-profit foundation to solve mass transit problems.

People who stay on a salary face the same kinds of problems. In a corporate setting some are called "office politics." But though you can't escape annoying details by staying on a salary, at least failure to handle details well won't make you starve when you work for someone else. Marketing, after-service, and manufacturing consume most of the time.

A Business Plan?

Most books on creating businesses say you should write a business plan — some words and numbers that not only state your business goal, but also say how you expect to get there.

Writing a plan forces people to think through all the issues of the business:

- What is your central idea?
- How will you deliver what you've promised?
- Who will sell your products?
- How will they (or you) persuade people to buy?
- Will you have enough money to survive while you're building up the business?

• Where do you want to be in six months, twelve months, one year, two years, and four years?

I think you should at least try writing a business plan — even if you have no idea whether you want to convert the idea that's in the back of your mind into a business. But try to write down how a chosen way of life might work. Talk about it with at least one or two other people. Trying to plan should force you to think about questions you had sought to gloss over. Or it may illuminate why you're avoiding setting yourself up independently and help you rethink your goals. If you're developing a partnership with someone else, at least making some notes toward a business plan is indispensable to building consensus on where you are going.

Orthodox business-planning courses really can be helpful. Matthew Reich, who founded Old New York Beer Company, had worked in the corporate-planning section of the Hearst Corporation. While there, he took an IBM course titled "How to Write a Strategic Plan." He says he followed the directions in the course almost exactly in writing the plan for his own business. If you can't take a business school–type course, additional resources for business planning appear in Appendix B.

Think realistically about how long it will take to make your business succeed. How soon will you be able to sell your services to the kinds of people whom you think should buy them? A general rule of thumb for professional services businesses such as those of lawyers and artists is that you'll spend the first year looking around like crazy for business, the second year you'll work like crazy to do the business you've got and find more, then in the third or fourth year you may learn whether you're going to make any money. Other kinds of businesses take longer — Chris Whittle's 13–30 Corp. took eight years to become solidly profitable. Others take less.

Don't assume you're so smart you'll succeed more quickly than others in your field. The only way you can be confident you'll be making a good living within a year is if you're able to line up two or three solid, reliable clients before you quit your current job. And lots of clients who talk like they'll be solid and reliable turn out to be less interested when the time comes to put up real money.

But don't be too fearful, either. You can cut your living expenses substantially if necessary to get a business off the ground. Just the elimination of commuting and meals at work can make big steps toward balanced budgets. And the government doesn't get to withhold income or Social Security tax from the money you make in self-employment. (See chapter 10 for details on using your new tax status effectively.)

Recognize that there's a grind ahead of you, but don't let it make you too cautious. "It's best to start a business when you're still a little naïve," says Steve Belkin, whose Transnational Corporation is now one of the nation's leading group-travel companies. "If I'd known what I know now, I'd have been too intimidated." Belkin is glad he went into business for himself, and so are most others who've been through the struggle.

Hardly any businesses develop as their business plans say they will, so having a business plan is much less important than having a clear central idea — the idea you write on the back of a business card. Try to write a plan, even if all you want to do is to move to the mountains of Colorado and live as simply as possible. You'll certainly want to complete the attempt if you intend to borrow money from a bank or ask others to invest in you. But if you're not going outside for money and you never complete the business plan, that's no great disaster. The main point is to think about your goals and how you can achieve them.

How to Lose $250,000 with an Elegant Business Plan

You can write a professional-sounding business plan and persuade hotshot investors to put money behind it, but that doesn't guarantee success. In fact, fashions among professional investors seem to change with the seasons even more than among the general public. You'll handle your business better if you think it through on the basis of your own instincts than if you trust someone or some technique because it is "professional."

Getting the form of a business plan "right" can persuade people to believe when they should see the flaws in the business's substance. For example, Bruce wanted to set up a fashion company. His father was a Wall Street attorney. Bruce had worked as a fashion model in high school and college, then became a financial analyst for an investment bank after graduating from college. He went to Harvard Business School and worked as assistant to the president of a major Seventh Avenue fashion company between his first and second years of school. His business plan was used as a case for study at the Business School before he had shipped his first product. It contained fourteen pages of financial projections that showed the company would make $167,173 profit in its second year. (Computers are great for producing impressive-looking financial projections.) He raised $250,000 from successful business-people, and his father's legal connections produced legal documents for him that might have cost $25,000 if prepared for a bigger business.

The year after business school, Bruce's own high-fashion Seventh Avenue showroom prominently displayed his name. He even had a good idea that could be written on the back of a business card: he would produce "a 'designer' line of clothing to fit the lifestyle of professional women." While he was working as a financial analyst, Bruce and his friends on Wall Street had noticed that the women's clothes that fit the subdued demands of serious business showed much less style than they could. He felt that Seventh Avenue didn't understand young professional businesswomen, and he could create an important company by serving their needs.

Bruce's first year's line got good reviews and sold well, but his business foundered on exactly the kinds of problems that a business plan is supposed to uncover. Bruce sought to be both his firm's president and its designer. He wanted to run virtually the entire business himself. He would design a line of clothes, manage its production at subcontract shops, and handle sales. Practically no one had ever done that successfully in the Seventh Avenue world, and Bruce soon found out why. People outside business school often don't behave exactly as business school graduates would like. "The production vendors would always say that the product would cost a certain price and be delivered on a certain date," he recalls. "Invariably the actual price would be substantially higher and the shipment would be late." So even when sales met his projections, profits didn't.

In his second year of business, reviewers praised his designs. But, "the people I was dealing with just practiced different ethics from what I was used to," he says. "People would promise an order and then not deliver. I couldn't understand why they wouldn't just tell me that they didn't want to buy the product."

The business plan called for sales of $300,000 in the second year's fall season. Bruce actually sold $50,000 worth. He closed the business. His investors got nothing but a tax loss. Today Bruce is back on Wall Street, creating mergers and acquisitions of other people's companies.

In retrospect, Bruce admits that he never liked the "team concept" of running a business. Perhaps that's why he didn't look for the business partner he needed in the first place.

Bruce's combination of talents was unusual. Probably he could have been either a good president or a good principal designer for a company. But no one can do everything. And attempting to do everything just made everything enormously difficult. "If I was in a bad mood, everyone's morale would suffer," he says.

Bruce could pull the details of the business together into a business-school–style plan. But he couldn't make the business succeed when it couldn't deliver on the plan and its entrepreneur lacked the temperament he needed.

Accomplishing Your Task: Should You Have Employees?

Bruce suffered because he entered a field where he needed both partners and employees, and he wasn't prepared to manage those relationships. In plenty of other businesses you don't need employees and you can get by without partners. And you may find you're better off without the "help" that a regular employee would give you.

Legally, you can set yourself up as a one-person business fairly simply. Just keep careful track of income and expenses and make estimated tax payments to the government every quarter, and you'll be all right. (Any accountant can give you details.)

But when you hire someone to work for you, the U.S. and state governments make life hard. You may become liable for federal withholding tax, social security tax, state tax, unemployment tax, workmen's compensation insurance, and other insurance payments. Other countries such as Japan and Germany exempt small businesses from many paperwork requirements, but in the United States it's not uncommon for a business taking on its first five-day-a-week employee to also take on a one-day-a-week part-time bookkeeper because of the increased paperwork.

In addition, supervising employees takes enormous amounts of time — especially if you haven't defined what you want them to do. Employees rarely figure out what they're supposed to do without being clearly told.

The majority of independent people should employ at least clerical help: your time is probably worth more in pursuits other than typing and filing. But you should probably call the people who work for you *independent contractors* — independent businesspeople from whom you're buying services — rather than employees. Just tell them you're hiring them on that basis and ask them to give you an invoice each time you pay them. A simple piece of paper with the word *invoice* at the top is sufficient. You need not do government paperwork when you employ independent contractors — though you still need to comply with safety laws.

When you hire people, whether as independent contractors or ordinary employees, avoid these three mistakes:

1. Hiring too quickly. Many people hire the first seemingly appropriate person who shows up. They should usually interview at least five people for the simplest jobs to learn who is around.
2. Underestimating the quality of people you can attract. Many people who know they need typing fail to consider that for the same money they could hire someone who can do more than just type. If your business is interesting, you may be surprised at who wants to work for you. One person I know runs a consulting business from his home and employs three poorly paid part-time secretaries. All are college graduates and together they make up for his own failure to keep the business organized.
3. Failing to check references. Many people are better at selling themselves than they are at doing work. Be sure to call the people who they say will vouch for them.

It may pay to advertise even the simplest job. And write down a description of its duties and the ideal person for it. You'll avoid headaches in the future.

How About a Partner?

As a general rule, it's a good idea to find a partner in any but the smallest business. At least talk to a few potential partners. If people don't want to be your partner, perhaps they have recognized something you haven't about the viability of your idea.

Many people don't believe they're temperamentally suited to be anyone's partner. As Bruce discovered, the kind of person who doesn't form partnerships easily may be the kind of person who fails in businesses normally run by partnerships.

Some people get partners by giving part of their businesses to employees. Many entrepreneurs do that too readily, though. Entrepreneurs assume that because owning stock in the company motivates people like them, owning stock in the company will motivate subordinates. Frequently this just isn't true. The test is: will the employee sacrifice for the equity? If an employee wants to take part of a raise in company stock or purchase the stock outright, consider giving it to him. But don't assume that owning a share in your business will make him loyal unless you have evidence that it will. Stock-owning employees can wind up quitting jobs, and the entrepreneur has to buy back the stock with money he can't afford to spend.

Manufacturing and Your Business

Virtually everyone will be involved with some kind of manufacturing, even if it's only the printing of brochures or reports, so you must work well with manufacturing people.

But manufacturing consumes a declining share of a business's resources today. Machines can do most of the work, and what the machines can't do can often be sent abroad to be done for less than it can be done at home.

You can make a profit selling a manufactured good (such as Brett Johnson's painter's caps). And if you're a commercial artist or a business consultant, a surprising share of your success will depend on relationships with printers and sometimes other manufacturing professionals who can make your work look good. Moreover, the demand for quality at the right price has made high-quality manufacturing more important today than ever before, and if you want to make a career in manufacturing, there are opportunities.

But the pressure on manufacturers over the last several decades has meant that there are thousands of manufacturing companies and experienced manufacturing people looking to do subcontract work and lacking enough business to keep them fully occupied. Unless you are a trained engineer, you're more likely to make a profit by conceiving a product to be manufactured by someone else and then getting it marketed properly than from making things yourself a little bit better or cheaper than others.

Learn to work with manufacturers. Seek out companies with the right combination of quality and price. But don't try to make products yourself until you're sure you can't get a better deal by contracting out the production.

Your Role in the Service Economy

Today, many businesses that look like manufacturing companies are really marketing and service companies. Old New York Beer Company's beer is actually produced by a subcontractor in Utica, New York, for instance. Entrepreneur Matthew Reich wants to build a brewery on the West Side of Manhattan, but if it succeeds there, it will do so because of the profits and increased sales due to brewery tours, not because Reich brews beer better than the subcontractor. Reich spends his time worrying about whether the managers of Upper West Side 7–11 stores are giving Heineken better display than his beer.

Service is a growing share of the economy. Many people's businesses consist of providing services: law, travel agenting, computer programming, real estate brokerage, polling for politicians, and so on. Most stores are service businesses first and sales businesses second. The proprietor's job is to find and make available the products the consumer wants and present them in a way that will let him recognize that he wants them. Machines can't usually perform customer service — you or someone you hire must do it. Crowd Caps couldn't easily automate the service for its distributors.

Occasionally you can subcontract customer service or leave it to your distributors, but you yourself will still have to provide service to the subcontractors and distributors — explaining how to use your product, taking care of units that either are or seem to be defective, et cetera.

Remember that "The customer is always right." Service doesn't consist simply of getting the product into shape where the customer *could* use it properly; it means helping him use it regardless of how different he may be from your ideal of a customer. If you run a consulting firm that produces reports for the government, "service" means satisfying the officials who OK your grants.

Quality Control

Regardless of who does manufacturing and service, however, you as the boss are in charge of quality control — making sure that things don't often go wrong.

There's one major principle of quality control: *You don't achieve quality primarily by exhorting people to be more careful, but by hiring careful people in the first place and keeping track of every mistake that occurs, how it came about, and what can be done in the future to avoid similar errors.* I'm always amazed at how few businesses — in the United States, anyway — bother to keep track of their mistakes. Only when you know what's going wrong can you figure out how to fix it, either by educating or eliminating a problem supplier, employee, or distributor.

Let the Market Set Your Prices

If you've defined your business clearly, you can probably figure out how to price and deliver your services by looking at others providing similar services.

Don't be creative in pricing unless you have a very good reason. You'll want your fees, at least officially, to equal the industry norm. But of course, you may also offer discounts when you realize a discount will win a job for you.

Selling and Marketing

Marketing — letting other people know about you and convincing them that they should give you money for your work — is for most people the toughest part of establishing themselves in their chosen field. Even if your chosen trade involves a standard method of marketing — showing wares at fashionable showrooms for Bruce's clothing business, for instance — there's no guarantee it will work for you. It may fail even if you have a great business idea that will ultimately make you rich. And if your profession normally cultivates the idea that its members don't sell themselves — say, you're a veterinarian or a psychiatrist — marketing can be even tougher because your professional training may leave you with little understanding of how it's done.

"The most unpleasant part of starting out on my own was the

amount of time it took to get money coming in on a regular basis,'' says a lawyer who has had an independent practice for almost two years. "You go month after month when you sort of race everybody to the bank. You read in magazines that the average lawyer makes $50,000 and you say, 'What was I doing making $14,500 last year?' "

Your key marketing objective is to communicate clearly what you can do, to people who could benefit by buying it. Even if you can hire a full-time sales and marketing manager, you'll wind up spending an enormous amount of your time on marketing for the first year or two. While there are one (or at most, a few) right ways to make things and to deliver any given service, there's usually no single right way to market it. You can only try several different ways — usually all at once — and see which works.

If your budget won't let you spend a great deal of time on long-term marketing efforts, expect to take many jobs in your first year at far below market rates just because they're easy to sell. The lawyer whose business is just now coming alive started his practice by taking a job as associate counsel for an established firm. The firm required him to work three days a week for $125 — about $5 an hour — and gave him free use of the office the other two days a week.

If you're setting up a profession, don't fail to tell all your friends and acquaintances that you're available for the right kind of work. And it will help if you can feel comfortable calling strangers, telling them what you do, and gently suggesting that perhaps you might be able to help them. "I ask consultants how they got their first jobs, and they always tell me: 'Cold calls, that's the only way to do it,' " says a man who counsels entrepreneurs.

If you want to make your business grow, think seriously about hiring a professional salesperson with a track record. Don't assume that you're too small to attract someone good by placing an ad in the *Wall Street Journal* or whatever publication serves your industry. Salesmen change jobs frequently, and many look for opportunities with new companies. But plan to interview at least ten people before hiring anyone. Check references. And don't forget that you must still devote a lot of your own time to sales and marketing regardless of who you've hired. Ultimately, everyone who hopes to get anything useful done must be a salesman.

Cost–Effective Advice: Accountants, Bankers, and Lawyers

Relationships with accountants, bankers, and lawyers deserve an important place in the plans of every creative person. Each is a vital — and often remarkably inexpensive — source of support that can help your projects succeed.

Choosing a Tax Adviser

Tax time is a good time to start selecting advisers. Most people should have someone else prepare their tax return, because a good preparer will save more money than he costs on almost anybody's taxes.

One friend of mine didn't bother filing a tax form one year because he was working full-time on a business idea and so had only $3,000 in income. He had a wife and a baby, and was living off past earnings. He wasn't required to file a return. The next year he was still in what might be called a "development mode" — gross earnings had risen to only $11,000. But he had to file a tax return, and he employed an accountant to do it. The accountant pointed out that he was eligible for an "earned income tax credit" for the year he hadn't filed. Even though he hadn't sent a penny to the IRS, he received a "refund" check for nearly $400, which left a nice bonus after paying the accountant's $150 fee for both years. And he got good planning and record-keeping advice in the bargain.

Don't scrimp on accountants' fees. There are literally hundreds of thousands of accountants in the United States, and most of them do some tax preparation and accounting for individuals. Fees vary enormously and so does quality. Often a mass-market tax preparer such as H&R Block will fill in forms for $30, while a big accounting firm located on a higher floor of the same building will charge $450 to do essentially the same work. (The big firm may get some work from professionals whose companies use the firm as their regular auditor. The companies may pay the preparation fees as a company benefit.)

H&R Block provides adequate tax help for many people who live on salaries, but a relationship with H&R Block won't benefit you when you want to start a business or buy some real estate. If you're living on a salary, you can probably find an accountant who will prepare your taxes for $100 or so. Many charge more and are well worth it for many people. Don't be afraid to ask about fees. You can consult with an accountant for relatively little money.

Look for an accountant just as you would look for a doctor or a plumber: ask friends, especially friends you consider financially savvy, to recommend one. Deal *only* with a licensed C.P.A.

Be sure to talk to an accountant if you are launching any business endeavor that will involve more than a few thousand dollars — even if it's nothing more than buying a two-family house. An accountant will show you how to set up your books for a fee that may be $50 or less. That's a good investment no matter how strapped you may be for cash. At this meeting you should also ask the accountant whether he advises you to use the *one-write system* of bookkeeping, which will cost perhaps $200 to set up but can save more time for most small businesses than a computer.

Why Bankers Are So Bankerly

Your banker will be the most cautious of all the advisers you'll work with — indeed, perhaps of all the *people* you'll work with — but you can gain more from making a banker comfortable with you than from building a relationship with any other person.

Julio Caro, a successful Manufacturers Hanover Trust banker who left to set up a film company, notes that nothing can do more to make you rich than learning to make a banker feel at ease giving you money. Bankers are cautious for good reasons. Banking is the lowest of low-margin businesses. Banks borrow one person's money, paying 6 to 11 percent for it, and lend it to someone else, who pays 9 to 18 percent. Unless the bank supplies lots of services (the processing of checks or credit card vouchers, for example), the bank must usually subsist on a "spread" — the difference between the interest rate paid to the depositor and the interest rate charged to the borrower — of 3 to 4 percent or so. If a bank nets 90 cents a year for each $100 it has lent out, it's doing well. If just one deal goes really sour, it can wipe out the profits from a hundred good deals — and it can ruin a banker's career.

Banks want to put their money in the hands of people like you because that's how they make their money. But if the amount is significant, they must make *very* sure that the money will come back. If you have capital — either some savings of your own, some money someone else has invested in your business, or some accumulated assets such as equity in your home or another business — you'll probably be able to get some kind of business loan fairly easily. In fact, almost anyone who has held a good job for a year or two can probably get a mortgage loan. But don't look for a loan made according to a formula (unless your business is very small). "Bankers feel they are in a people business," notes Caro. "You can go a long way with contacts — any contacts."

Have you ever lent money to friends? If you have, you probably cared more about what kind of people the borrowers were than about how much their homes or cars were worth. You asked yourself, "Is Joe the kind of guy who pays his debts?" Bankers are often like that. A banker who knows your mother or who knows that you're an upstanding person because you've gone to church with him for a year may well give you a much better hearing than a banker who sees a total stranger sitting in the plastic-covered chair in front of him. Even if your only "contact" is that the banker's third cousin knew you in college, that can help a lot.

Face-to-face communication is vital in a good banking relationship (except occasionally when you *want* to borrow from a computer; see "Do You Want to Borrow from a Banker or a Computer?" below). If your bank has no loan officers sitting on the floor of its branches, find out where they are located, go there, and meet some of them — or else find another bank.

Visit numerous banks. You'll probably have better success at a smaller bank if you're a bright person with a risky-sounding deal. Small banks don't have to be as bureaucratic about medium-sized deals as the multinationals.

In other kinds of interviews, the interviewer may see his major job as making you feel relaxed. In a banking interview, recognize that your job is to make the banker feel relaxed. Don't be pushy and don't quibble if the banker wants to charge you a fee up front. Respectfully *ask* if there is flexibility in his terms. (And be sure to talk to a few banks before you settle on one, so that you're sure you're being charged a competitive fee and interest rate. After you've talked to a few banks, you can go back and try to negotiate more aggressively with the banker you think you want to deal with.)

Even if your business is a corporation, recognize that the bank will expect you to guarantee repayment personally. Banks have been burned too often by entrepreneurs who got bored with reasonably healthy businesses and left them — leaving the banks with the tough job of collecting the loan on the basis of the underlying assets.

Show that you've thought about how you will repay the banker if your business fails. Show that you can bring in other accounts. (If you're going to own property, ask if the banker would like you to send new tenants to his bank. If you'll be operating stores, ask under what circumstances he would like to provide financing for customers.) Sometimes you may even want your tenants or potential tenants to provide evidence of their creditworthiness that you can show to the banker.

A good banker knows how to structure deals so he'll be covered and you can make money. "The only way you can get rich is by working with a banker," notes Julio Caro. "He's not going to get rich on your deal, so make sure you show him you'll take care of him." If the business fails, the bank will probably give you more time to repay the loan, but don't forget that you *must* repay everything. "Get the bank out and they'll probably be willing to back you again," says Julio. "Banks are always looking for you to have a way out for them."

You should not apply for a loan if your banker advises against it. You don't want your record to indicate that you applied for a loan that the bank considered imprudent.

Personalities in Banking

No two banks will approach a deal the same way. Kit Barry, a dealer in nineteenth-century commercial art and a real estate entrepreneur in Brattleboro, Vermont (whom I mentioned in chapter

1), borrows from four of the five banks in his town. "I think that every bank has its own personality. I wanted to know what the personalities of each bank were and be able to appeal to them."

Barry finds that some bankers basically understand simple mortgages best and may have the best rates. (Savings banks and savings and loan associations have traditionally specialized in this kind of deal.) Other banks are more comfortable with renovations and are more willing to lend to cover the negative cash flow that will exist while the building has no tenants.

If you have less than a couple hundred thousand dollars in assets, you probably can't spread your business among more than two or three banks and expect to know anyone at the banks well. But Barry's experience has shown the advantages of knowing who's around.

Generally Barry's commercial art business hasn't been "bankable." Barry travels to shows all over the country buying and selling "trade cards" — the cards nineteenth-century businessmen used to promote their wares. Because he kept his best discoveries for himself, his cash flow was always weak. Brattleboro bankers didn't understand what he was doing and didn't want to learn.

Two years ago, when interest rates were high and the survival of many savings banks was in doubt, a savings bank in Brattleboro hired a New York banker to turn its banking style around. Barry went to see him within a few weeks of his arrival. "It turns out he knows exactly what I'm doing. All his summers when he was in school he came up to work for an antique dealer in Vermont." Barry realized that the new man was looking for local businessmen who could be his "golden boys" — people who would reliably borrow and repay large sums of money. Barry was an ideal candidate. Unlike other bankers, this guy actually knew that the collection of papers in Barry's house was worth several hundred thousand dollars. Within a few months, Barry had a $40,000 line of credit for his business plus $375,000 that he's using to buy and renovate an early-twentieth-century office building and ballroom in downtown Brattleboro. Barry had connected with a bank whose personality was right for his business.

Do You Want to Borrow from a Banker or a Computer?

Occasionally you want to avoid any serious "relationship" with a banker. Recently banks have cut costs and sometimes improved the quality of their small-scale lending by turning much of the decision-making over to machines. You fill in a form, and either a clerk gives you some prescribed number of points for each answer or enters your answers into a computer. Either way, a computer-generated formula determines whether you get the loan.

When you build up credit lines as I described in chapter 3, you're essentially arranging to borrow from a computer. Most large banks handle most personal loans the same way. If you have a decent salary and good payment records on everything you've previously borrowed, and you don't need too much money, computerized lending can be great.

Graduating to a Human-Being Banker

Even if your business is much too small to interest a good loan officer today, start looking for a good human banker right away. Try to talk to him about your loan or credit card applications and your business dreams. Many good bankers enjoy talking about ideas outside the normal course of car loans, home mortgages, and bounced checks that cross their desks in a local branch.

You can learn a great deal about doing business from conversations with a good banker. He may be able to get you a better deal on a loan or a credit card than the computer. Some local banks, for example, charge lower interest on credit card bills than the big banks that send you direct-mail ads, and if you can get a large line of credit from one of them, you may save a couple hundred dollars a year over the cost of a "Premium Visa" account through a national bank. Most important, by starting a personal relationship, you're starting to establish your creditworthiness for the future.

Eventually, you need at least one and probably several human bankers. Computers do a fine job of evaluating whether your salary and repayment history indicate you will repay a personal loan, but they can't yet understand a real estate deal or a business proposition. When you have a need for money that allows you to explain to a human being exactly why he need not have the *slightest* worry that the loan might not be repaid, then it's time to go looking for a real banker. Finding a good one can ultimately make you rich.

Negotiating with a Lawyer

Finding a lawyer for anything but routine work is more like getting married or buying a house than it is like hiring a plumber or even an accountant. A badly written contract can destroy a business, and once you've involved a lawyer in your affairs, you may have difficulty divorcing yourself from him. Thus when you hire a lawyer, you want a partner you can trust — but part of that trusting relationship may be tough negotiations between you and him to create a fee structure and communications channel you can both live with. Speak to several lawyers before you hire one, and never hire one you're uncomfortable with.

New York attorney Jeffrey Drummond urges that you never go to a lawyer until you're sure you know what you want to do. "Start with a defined goal. No matter how broad this goal is, you must remember that you are there to work out a deal and you want the lawyer to handle the details."

The lawyer's function is to know — or find out — the legal details relevant to your transaction. While almost everyone needs an accountant and a banker — and it need not cost you much to employ them — you generally hire a lawyer only when you have a specific need for one. Try to centralize your business with one or two lawyers if possible, but also remember that different lawyers are good for different jobs — and a $40-an-hour lawyer who's good enough to do an eviction for you may not be good enough to prepare an important partnership agreement.

Once you know what you want to do, the key task is to find a lawyer who

- knows how to do what you need,
- cares for your best interests,
- explains things so you understand them, and
- charges affordable fees.

Don't underestimate how much of the law you understand. The first test of the quality of a lawyer's help is whether his comments agree with your common sense. If you're planning a major business deal, a lawyer should be willing to give you thirty minutes to two hours as an initial interview before you've committed yourself to spending any money with him. (If you end up hiring him, he'll probably bill you for this time.) You describe the deal; he gives you ideas on how to handle problems.

Drummond suggests five questions to ask yourself:

- Does he ask for the facts, and organize as he goes along?
- Does he really listen to what you say?
- Does he take notes?
- Does he respond with ideas about what to do as you talk?
- Does he mention relevant experience that you think valuable?

Look for *judgment.* You want someone who will know what to do and how to represent your interest even when there are no clear rules. You should have growing confidence in the lawyer as you talk to him.

If a friend is a lawyer, consider hiring him. You probably know whether you can trust a friend far better than you can know whether to trust a stranger. The key question in considering a friend is whether he has enough experience and knowledge to handle your particular problem. You don't necessarily need a friend who has handled exactly your kind of deal before, but you need someone who shows enough general knowledge to demonstrate that he understands the issues and also has an honest willingness to admit what he doesn't know and to learn about it.

Talk freely about fees. Most lawyers will charge $50 to $150 per hour. But a lawyer whose time isn't fully booked will often work fixed-price deals where he bills fewer hours than he actually devotes to a project.

Typically a lawyer will ask for a "retainer" — a deposit you make at the beginning, which he draws against as he completes work for you. This is standard procedure, but it is also expensive. Often you can work out much easier payment plans. Matthew Reich of Old New York Beer Company had his attorneys work "on speculation" — they would be paid only if he succeeded in raising money to start the business. I got a lawyer to accept a share in the partnership instead of cash fees when I set up a magazine a few years ago.

If a lawyer believes in you, it's well worthwhile for him to negotiate with you. Legal services typically account for 2 to 5 percent of the cost of setting up a creative business — and the lawyer will get even more in regular fees as your deal becomes a going concern. At minimum you should get a discount on the lawyer's services for the period when the business is being formed. As a cost-control move, you should also ask the lawyer to bill you monthly — and review the charges carefully. Complain when work costs more than estimated and there's no good reason.

Finally, never go to a lawyer for business advice. Lawyers — unlike bankers and real estate agents and sometimes accountants — can earn very good money even if they are terrible businessmen, so they often think they know how business should be conducted, when all they know is how to guarantee a steady flow of legal fees.

A Tax Primer for the Not-Yet Rich

A few months ago I figured out my total tax bracket for the first time. I was shocked. Forty-seven percent of every dollar of additional taxable income I earn goes to the U.S., New York State, or New York City governments.

I'd always avoided knowing the tax rate on each additional dollar I earned. I was vaguely aware that the truth would be painful, but I could ignore it fairly easily because there's such a big gap between the *average* share of my salary and other income that I pay in taxes and the *marginal* tax bracket that I face on each *additional* dollar of income. Deductions reduce my taxes substantially. Despite my high bracket, I actually pay a total of only about 20 percent of my income in direct income taxes. But if I earned another dollar of income, I'd immediately lose 47 percent of it. And if I found a dollar in new deductions, I'd immediately have 47 cents more to spend however I wanted.

Forty-seven percent! A 47 percent total tax bracket means an additional $6,000 in income nets me only $3,180. Just by buying a larger condominium, whose interest payments would shelter an additional $10,000 a year, I would gain as much in tax benefits as I could gain in spendable cash from an $8,000-a-year raise.

Creating a Tax Strategy

I suspect most people are like me: they're paying perhaps 20 percent of their total incomes in taxes today. They don't know how much tax they're paying on each additional dollar of income, and they have only a vague idea of how much they could save by developing an intelligent tax strategy.

But total *marginal* tax brackets are high for almost everyone, and they'll remain high for most people under virtually all the proposed tax "simplification" and "reform" proposals in Congress as this is written. Everyone who hasn't developed a tax strategy — a plan for how they'll manage their finances to minimize the tax bite — is almost certainly giving up thousands of dollars a year.

Thus people should calculate their total marginal tax bracket. Most will find they need to calculate their bracket at least two ways, as I'll discuss below. Once you know your bracket, plan to save money by generating the specific kinds of deductions that will benefit you the most.

This chapter will help you with the ins and outs of the tax laws and provide a basic guide to creating a strategy.

Planning for Tax Changes

Can you prepare a tax strategy if Washington is still buzzing with tax "reform" talk? Can you use the advice in this chapter even if Congress has changed the rules since it was written?

Absolutely. Some current tax-simplification ideas in Washington may cut marginal tax brackets a bit and thus make tax-planning mistakes less costly, but no proposals I've seen would dramatically change the need for tax planning. None would ruin the financial plans of ordinary people who designed intelligent strategies based on the old laws. And most would not render any of the advice in this chapter obsolete. You need tax planning in a time of tax "reform" as much as at any other time.

If tax "simplification" and "reform" remain big issues when you read this, don't let confusing rumors in the newspapers prevent you from creating a tax strategy. Just try to sort out what the newspapers are saying, and be sure your tax moves would still make sense if Congress enacted the most widely talked about tax changes. The only real danger is buying property whose value depends on your ability to deduct the local taxes you'll pay on it (see chapters 3 and 5). If you make sure that your real estate investments give you *real* value, you can generally assume that any appropriate tax move discussed here will benefit you — no matter what they do in Washington.

Calculating Your Total Tax Bracket

The first step in creating a tax strategy is knowing, at least roughly, your tax bracket. Then you can plan your spending and investing so it avoids the taxes that are hurting — or will hurt — you most.

Check your last tax return and find out what your taxable income was. The chart below will show what your marginal tax bracket was *at the federal level only*. If rates have changed substantially, you'll of course have to find a new tax chart. (You can use the one that comes with the instructions for filing your tax return.) But the importance of your tax bracket won't have changed.

Don't be reassured if your bracket seems fairly modest when you find it in the chart below. You still must add in Social Security, state, and local taxes, and when they're included, it's a safe bet your bracket will hurt.

Here are charts showing marginal federal tax rates on 1985 taxable income:

Single Taxpayers Filing Status Box 1			**Unmarried Heads of Household** Filing Status Box 4		
If taxable income (Form 1040, line 37) is over	But not over	Marginal tax bracket is	If taxable income (Form 1040, line 37) is over	But not over	Marginal tax bracket is
$0	$2,390	–0–	$0	$2,390	–0–
2,390	3,540	11%	2,390	4,580	11%
3,540	4,580	12%	4,580	6,760	12%
4,580	6,760	14%	6,760	9,050	14%
6,760	8,850	15%	9,050	12,280	17%
8,850	11,240	16%	12,280	15,610	18%
11,240	13,430	18%	15,610	18,940	20%
13,430	15,610	20%	18,940	24,460	24%
15,610	18,940	23%	24,460	29,970	28%
18,940	24,460	26%	29,970	35,490	32%
24,460	29,970	30%	35,490	46,520	35%
29,970	35,490	34%	46,520	63,070	42%
35,490	43,190	38%	63,070	85,130	45%
43,190	57,550	42%	85,130	112,720	48%
57,550	85,130	48%	112,720	——	50%
85,130	——	50%			

Married Taxpayers Filing Joint Returns, and Qualifying Widows and Widowers Filing Status Box 2 or 5			Married Taxpayers Filing Separate Returns Filing Status Box 3		
If taxable income (Form 1040, line 37) is over	But not over	Marginal tax bracket is	If taxable income (Form 1040, line 37) is over	But not over	Marginal tax bracket is
$0	$3,540	–0–	$0	$1,770	–0–
3,540	5,720	11%	1,770	2,860	11%
5,720	7,910	12%	2,860	3,955	12%
7,910	12,390	14%	3,955	6,195	14%
12,390	16,650	16%	6,195	8,325	16%
16,650	21,020	18%	8,325	10,510	18%
21,020	25,600	22%	10,510	12,800	22%
25,600	31,120	25%	12,800	15,560	25%
31,120	36,630	28%	15,560	18,315	28%
36,630	47,670	33%	18,315	23,835	33%
47,670	62,450	38%	23,835	31,225	38%
62,450	89,090	42%	31,225	44,545	42%
89,090	113,860	45%	44,545	56,930	45%
113,860	169,020	49%	56,930	84,510	49%
169,020	———	50%	84,510	———	50%

State and local income taxes are largely based on federal taxes, so you may be able to just add them to your federal tax bracket to get your total bracket. (Check your local tax forms to get the correct numbers.)

Traditionally, state and local taxes have been deductible on that year's federal tax returns, however. Though Congress may have abolished this deduction by the time you read this, it may still be in force. If so, you should add less than the total state and local tax rate to the federal rate. If your federal bracket is 30 percent and your state has an income tax of 7.5 percent, for instance, you'll be able to save 30 cents on your federal taxes for every dollar you pay in state taxes — unless the federal government ends the deduction before your next return is due. Thus you can probably assume your state tax will only cost you 5.25 percent of each additional dollar of income you earn. (That's the state tax rate of 7.5

percent multiplied by the 70 percent share of your income that your federal tax bracket allows you to keep.) Thus your combined federal and state tax bracket would be 35.25 percent.

Calculating your tax bracket becomes really horrendous when you start to take Social Security taxes into account — if your income is less than $39,600 a year. Social Security taxes affect you quite differently from ordinary federal, state, and local taxes.

In principle, Social Security taxes sound modest: if you're on a payroll, you pay a tax of just 7.05 percent, effective on no more than $39,600 of income. That sounds like no more than many state and local taxes, and far less than the federal income tax. In reality, your boss also pays 7.05 percent if you're an employee. (The self-employed pay Social Security tax at a higher rate — currently 11.8 percent — because they have no employer to make a "contribution.") But your boss's "contribution" comes out of your pocket even though you never see it. Anyone who runs a business thinks of the whole cost of an employee when he thinks about hiring or giving a raise. When I say my total taxes are 20 percent of my income, I'm ignoring the hidden part of the Social Security tax. When I include it, I have to recognize that taxes take a significantly larger bite.

Moreover, absolutely *nothing* is deductible from Social Security tax unless you're self-employed. For many this is the most vicious of all taxes. If a man is trying to support two infants, one of whom is chronically ill, and a wife who stays home to care for them, all on a salary of $22,000 a year, he has lots of income tax deductions and probably pays virtually no federal, state, or local income tax. But the government collects $1,650 in Social Security tax on his salary and $1,650 from his employer.

From a tax-planning point of view, this makes Social Security tricky. Unless you have a gross income greater than $39,600 (or whatever the maximum is for Social Security taxes by the time you read this), you have to calculate your total tax bracket two ways:

1. Excluding Social Security taxes. This number will indicate the benefits of tax-saving tactics such as real estate investments that create tax losses.
2. Including Social Security taxes. This number will indicate the benefits of tax-saving strategies such as getting your employer to provide tax-free benefits instead of a raise and, if part of

your income is from self-employment, spending money on items that are deductible as business expenses.

If your state or local income tax is calculated in a different way from the federal income tax, you may also want to calculate a separate total tax bracket for income that's treated differently by your state than by the federal government.

You may find that calculating your tax bracket is so complex that you can never finish the job. That's OK. Just *roughly* knowing your bracket is enough. But having an idea of your tax bracket is important. Your bracket tells you just how much you can gain through various tax-oriented maneuvers.

Should You Set a Tax-Savings Target?

Now that you know your tax bracket, think about what bracket you'd like to be in. Don't try to avoid paying taxes altogether; it's a waste of time to try to push your marginal federal tax bracket much below 20 percent (the bracket people reach with about $13,000 in taxable income). At that point you pay about $1,200 in federal income tax. If you find a worthwhile investment that pushes you below that level, great, but don't stay awake at night thinking about it.

On the other hand, you probably should look for opportunities to get your tax bracket down to 35 percent or less. There are many good opportunities for tax shelter that can bring your tax bill down and produce long-term capital gains at the same time. Suppose your gross income is $38,000 a year. You might report $32,000 or so in taxable income without any tax planning. But a real estate investment and one or two other intelligent moves can fairly easily cut your taxable income to $20,000 or so. That means you'll cut your federal taxes alone by $3,600 a year — the equivalent of a $5,500-a-year or $450-a-month taxable raise — more if you take state and local taxes into account. And the smart actions to cut taxes should benefit you in other ways as well.

My own tax strategy is to find enough tax-favored investments to cut my bracket down to something more reasonable, but others may need totally different approaches.

• Ellen, a $28,000-a-year computer saleswoman, has just bought an $86,000 condominium and already has $11,000 in interest deductions on her income tax. Her total taxable income is only $16,000, so her total tax bracket excluding Social Security is only 23 percent. She doesn't need any more tax-advantaged investments. But including the real cost of Social Security taxes, her total tax bracket is 37 percent. She should still encourage her employer to give her tax-free benefits instead of more salary (pending tax-law changes might affect this). On the other hand, she should watch out for any suggestion that she become a self-employed salesperson to cut her taxes further: though self-employment would give her even more useful deductions, her medical insurance and similar benefits would no longer be fully paid by her employer and that might cancel out any advantage.

- Jim, a $24,000-a-year securities salesman who plans to return to business school, doesn't expect to remain where he is for long, so he won't buy real estate. But he is putting money in an Individual Retirement Account even though he has no interest in retirement yet. His total tax bracket excluding Social Security is 28 percent now. He'll take the money out when he's in business school. He'll pay a 10 percent penalty, but he knows his tax bracket will be zero when he's in business school, so even though he pays the penalty he'll save 18 percent of the money. He'll make more than $1,000 tax-free on three years of Individual Retirement Account contributions. (There are currently several proposals to increase the penalty, so consult an accountant before executing this strategy.)

- Joe, a business consultant whose practice is still small, grossed $40,000 last year. A lot of that went to pay for phone bills and computer supplies; Joe figures that his $40,000 gross allowed him to live roughly as a salaried person could live on $30,000. Joe has a family, owns the house in Massachusetts where he lives and works, and can take large deductions because he uses one of the house's seven rooms as an office. For tax purposes his income is only $22,000, and his total marginal tax bracket (excluding Social Security) is 22 percent. But because he's self-employed, he pays Social Security taxes directly. His Social Security payments of $2,360 a year are nearly twice as large as his federal income tax payments, and his total marginal tax bracket including Social Security taxes is nearly 34 percent. He doesn't worry about additional real estate tax shelters. Instead, he concentrates on arranging his spending so that as much as possible will be classifiable as business expenses — and thus deductible from Social Security taxes as well as from ordinary income taxes.

Though all these people have different strategies, they have something in common. They all *understand* taxes well enough to create their own strategies. Once you understand a little bit about taxes, saving money by finding tax deductions is easier and surer than obtaining money in most other ways.

Owning Your Home

Home ownership creates the simplest and in many ways best opportunities for tax savings. Mortgage interest and — at least as this is written — local real estate taxes are deductible. The mortgage interest deduction is most important because 99 percent of the payment you make on a mortgage for the first few years will be interest.

Moreover, you need pay no capital-gains tax on the profits from owning a home and selling it at a profit. The tax laws allow you to "roll over" any gain you make. As long as you reinvest in another, more expensive home within two years, you need pay no taxes. When you reach age fifty-five you'll be exempt from tax on up to $125,000 profit on the sale of your house, but you can only take this exemption once.

How a Side Business Affects Your Taxes

Part-time businesses — especially but not exclusively in real estate — can do even more to improve your tax position than home ownership. Most side businesses can be arranged to report either a loss or a smaller profit than the cash they produce would indicate. Real estate businesses are generally the best tax shelters because they generate enormous interest and depreciation deductions. But other businesses also offer benefits.

Suppose you've always been fascinated by art history. Consider setting yourself up as an art consultant, teaching and advising about art in addition to your full-time work as a corporate lawyer.

The Internal Revenue Service won't allow any deductions unless you're actually doing business: if you just talk about selling your art history advice, or if you just do a little bit of consulting that is incidental to a hobby, you can't deduct books about art history or the cost of attending art history lectures. But if you start lecturing on the subject and advising a local museum or private collector for money, and if you keep books and otherwise conduct the operation in a businesslike way, then you can legitimately call art history a business, and your art history–related payments are business expenses.

Unless you're in a tax-advantaged field such as real estate, you shouldn't start reporting an activity as a business unless you genuinely expect that you'll eventually report a profit on it. The IRS investigates taxpayers whose businesses always lose money yet never close down. People who declare that their gardens are "farms" face particularly close scrutiny. To achieve a presumption that your "business' is run for profit, you must show a profit in two years out of five. If you can't do that, you may face tough arguments from the tax man.

But even the IRS acknowledges that there are many legitimate deductions for people who run small businesses from their homes. The room where you once worked on art history as a hobby can be an office. When your business is making money you can deduct a portion of your mortgage payment plus depreciation (or rent) and home maintenance expenses. The rules about home offices are fairly strict, but not so strict that you can't meet the IRS's tests: the section of your house that is your office must be used exclusively for business. You must either use it to meet with clients or it must be your principal place of business. And you can't deduct more for the use of a home office than the income of the business less other expenses.

Similarly, transportation and tools used in your business are deductible expenses. If you fly to Ann Arbor, Michigan, where you attend an art history conference and also visit your mother, you should allocate some of the expense to personal affairs and some to business. By proving that your primary purpose was business, you can deduct the major expenses like airfare. For example, if you took a six-day trip and spent five days on business and one day visiting your mother, you may deduct the major expenses such as airfare, car rental, and hotel. Just make sure you don't deduct expenses for the one day you did not work. Even after allocating some of the expenses to personal affairs, your deduction will be substantial. A computer, office furniture, and bookshelves are all deductible (though you must be prepared to document that you used the computer primarily for your business).

Understanding Depreciation   The biggest complexity in tax deductions for a small business or a real estate investor — and the biggest source of major tax savings — is depreciation. Depreciation is an allowance for wear and tear on a durable product. When you make a major purchase that's designed to last — say, office furniture or some real estate — the government generally won't let you deduct the entire amount as a business expense right away. You must deduct only a portion of the value of the property each year — an amount that's more or less supposed to represent the extent to which the product is wearing out. Office furniture and most other business equipment is generally depreciable over five years, buildings over eighteen years.

Depreciation of large investments such as buildings creates enormous opportunities for tax savings. If you take reasonably good care of a building, it won't decline in value, it will increase in value. Yet the tax laws allow you to deduct an amount each year for depreciation. On a $100,000 building, for example, you can deduct approximately $9,000 in the year you buy it and about $9,000 the year after that.* Thus a real estate business will routinely report big losses to the government even when it's generating lots of cash for the buildings' owners. Even the depreciation generated by a one-room office in your home can result in a nice deduction from your taxable income.

When you sell a building, you must pay capital-gains tax on the difference between the depreciated value of the building and the price you sell it for. When you've owned the $100,000 building for two years, for instance, its depreciated value will be $82,000, but its real value is likely to be much more. If you then sell it for $150,000, you pay capital-gains tax on $68,000.

But long-term capital-gains rates are far below ordinary income rates. As this is written, capital-gains rates are only 40 percent of regular income rates. You can pay your capital-gains tax easily out of the profit on a successful sale. Or you can find some other way to defer the taxes again. The most successful investors simply keep deferring and deferring the taxes on their gains — all the while

*Based on a 1984 schedule, eighteen-year depreciation analysis. It is almost certain that this will change in 1986.

using their money to make more money. In principle their potential tax liability is increasing all the time, but in fact, smart, tax-advantaged investments will defer their taxes indefinitely.

Most small businesses can avoid even the inconvenience of having to depreciate items like filing cabinets a little at a time. There's a special privilege that lets small businesses deduct up to $5,000 a year in durable products they would ordinarily have to depreciate. This can be a real boon; the paperwork involved in depreciating a $250 desk would otherwise be an enormous headache. But watch out: there are special rules on the deductibility of computers and autos used partially in business and partially for ordinary life.

You report all this wheeling and dealing to the government on Schedule C, "Profit or Loss from a Business or Profession," or Schedule E, "Supplemental Income Schedule" (from rents and royalties, partnerships, estates, and trusts, and so on). Most people should be filing one of these forms: many worthwhile activities should be handled as businesses or professions. You can often report a loss while you're building the business up, and keep your taxable income down when you start making money.

Should You Be in Business Full-Time?

If the tax deductions available to entrepreneurs look good to you, you may be considering going into business for yourself full-time. But don't do that just for the tax deductions.

Self-employment does offer substantial deductions: a home office, travel costs, some books, and many other items can become deductible when they might not be deductible for an employee. But if self-employment is your only employment, you also lose important tax exemptions that you had as an employee. Employers can buy you medical insurance, life insurance, and even sports club memberships tax-free. When you become self-employed, most of those payments will come out of your income (though part of your medical insurance payment may be deductible as a medical expense).

From a tax point of view, it's best to stay on somebody's payroll so you can get benefits tax-free, but also derive a large share of your income from outside work so you can write off other expenses without fear that the IRS will claim you're only pretending to be in business.

Other Tax Tactics

Many people waste time and money trying to save on taxes. Most investments sold as "tax shelters" are a waste of money for most people. The most common are real estate partnerships of one sort or another. Somebody sets up a deal, and then instead of going to friends or big investors to finance it, he works out a plan with an investment company to let the investment company sell partnerships. Who do you think gets the better part of the deal, the buyers, or the guys who set it up? And if you get to write off more than you put in, you're likely to be signing a contract whose fine print says that if the organizer of the deal screws up, some bank can come after you for more money. But before the bank gets you, you'll have to settle up with the IRS. Who needs that kind of deal?

You'll do far better organizing and finding your own partnerships. But there are other tax shelters that while far less powerful than side businesses, still form essential parts of many good tax strategies.

Individual Retirement Accounts Individual Retirement Accounts are generally worth much of the hype they've generated in the media, though they're not nearly as powerful tax shelters as real estate investments and side businesses.

As you know, the government allows you to contribute $2,000 a year to an Individual Retirement Account and deduct that money from your income tax return. But you pay a penalty of 10 percent of the money withdrawn if you withdraw any of the money before age fifty-nine and a half, unless you're disabled. Also, you can't use the account as security for a loan without paying the same penalty you'd pay if you withdrew the money. (Obviously banks notice that your IRA is part of your balance sheet anyway and consider you more creditworthy because you've got it.)

If the only advantage of an IRA was that it let you shelter $2,000 a year in exchange for a promise not to touch it till age fifty-nine and a half, I wouldn't advise many young people to bother with IRAs. I don't want to wait around for profits I can't take till I'm almost sixty. But IRAs have an additional advantage: in addition to allowing you to take a deduction for money you put aside, they also allow your money to accumulate tax-free. For example, if you keep some of your money in a money-market fund or other fixed-income investment, you'll pay tax every year on that year's dividends. But if the money is in an IRA, you just keep accumulating dividends on top of dividends. You never pay any tax on them until you withdraw them. If you can keep your money invested for seven years or so, the tax savings from the sheltering of the dividends you're receiving will outweigh the penalty you'll then have to pay if you must take your money out.

The other highly publicized tax dodge, *tax-exempt bonds,* is principally useful for rich corporations and elderly millionaires. I'll discuss when it may be useful to you in the next chapter, but don't make it a key part of your tax strategy.

Trust Accounts for Children If you have kids, you've already started to worry about how you'll put them through college. You may have started putting money away. If you have, it should be in a trust account (sometimes called "an account under the Uniform Gifts for Minors Act").

Income received by trust accounts is considered the beneficiary's (i.e., the children's) income, not the parent's. So it's taxed at rates based on the beneficiary's income. For young children, that's probably zero.

Income will accumulate in a trust account just like it would in an Individual Retirement Account, but there's no penalty if you withdraw money from the account for the beneficiary's benefit. And because there's no penalty for early withdrawals, there's no bureaucracy involved if you want to shift money from one type of investment to another. The trust account remains completely tax-free until the kid's income is $2,390 a year.

There are currently proposals to change the trust laws, so consult an accountant before setting one up.

There are many other other fancy trusts you can read about in tax books, and your accountant can explain them to you someday when you have lots of money to shelter and you can afford to pay big legal fees. But until then, you can use the simple trust accounts available at any bank, mutual-fund company, or brokerage house.

Long-term Gains, Short-term Losses If you ever buy something — particularly stocks, bonds, or mutual-fund shares — that goes down, try to get rid of it quickly. But hang on to your successful buys for a while. The reason is the way the tax laws treat gains and losses.

Short-term capital gains and losses are fully taxable or deductible, just as if you had made or lost the money in business. But after a holding period — most recently, six months — these gains and losses become *long-term* capital gains and losses. Then they're taxable (or deductible) at much lower rates.

The idea is to sell the losers while they're still fully deductible and keep the winners till they're taxable as long-term gains. Suppose your total tax bracket is 40 percent and you buy $3,000 worth of two different stocks. Now suppose one of them doubles in price while the other company goes bankrupt and your stock becomes worthless. You could still make $70 or so in profit if you wrote off the loss as a short-term loss but kept the gain as a long-term gain and in a separate year. But be careful. If you sell them in the same year, you'll have to net them long-term versus short-term and then tax that difference. In this case you might wind up with nothing. If you are going to do this, know *all* the rules. Work with an accountant to determine your best strategy. Be wary of advice from your broker. In general, he isn't considering your tax welfare: he earns commissions when you buy and sell stocks.

In-kind Contributions to Charities   If you donate anything to a nonprofit organization, whether it's an old desk or the driving of a bunch of kids to a museum in your car, you can deduct the fair market value. It doesn't matter if the item wasn't useful to you. Automobile use, however, must be valued at a lower rate per mile than is used for business: recently the IRS allowed 12 cents per mile for charity driving, but 20.5 cents for business driving.

Taxes and Cash Flow

I suspect many people neglect tax planning because they can't immediately see the money it produces. But don't forget that you *can* arrange for an immediate increase in your paycheck anytime you do something that will cut your tax liability. You need *never* let your employer withhold more taxes from your paycheck than you're going to owe at the end of the year.

The purpose of withholding taxes is to guarantee that the government will get its money. Thus the purpose of the W-4 form you fill out as a new employee in any company is simply to give your employer an idea about an appropriate amount to withhold from your pay. I discussed this form in chapter 3. When it asks how many "exemptions" you want, you're encouraged to take one exemption for yourself and one for each dependent. But you can take any number that is likely to lead to a reasonable balance between the taxes withheld and the taxes you'll owe at the end of the year.

And if you do something — anything — during the year that will cut your liability, remember that you can ask your employer for a new W-4 form, take more exemptions, and get more money in your next paycheck.

On the other hand, if you start a side business that produces significant income, remember that you may be liable for quarterly estimated tax payments if you make so much that your ordinary withholding taxes don't amount to 80 percent of the taxes you'll owe at the end of the year.

Try to keep your withholding tax or estimated tax payments during the year close to the amount you'll owe at the end of the year. And whenever you do something that will dramatically cut your tax bill, reward yourself. Reduce your withholding tax or the amount of estimated taxes you pay by an appropriate amount.

For More Information

This chapter should get you started on a tax strategy. But somehow, the tax laws seem to be the most complex body of knowledge ever created by humanity. For further information, don't be afraid to look for help, either by paying an accountant or by buying an additional tax guide.

You'll benefit by paying regularly for an accountant's advice, but you should also do some research on your own. New York accountant Paul Fish says that some Internal Revenue Service publications are worthwhile, but you shouldn't count on them to show you innovative ways to save money. The booklet *Your Federal Income Tax* is highly regarded, and it's free. Of privately published income tax guides Fish recommends, *J. K. Lasser's Your Income Tax* remains the most thorough, and it's a good investment. Miller's *Personal Income Tax Guide* has useful worksheets. And a more technical, though still helpful, book is *Master Tax Guide,* published by Commerce Clearing House.

Unfortunately, virtually all publishers of private income tax "guides" seem to hire the same people to write the guides as the people who prepare the Internal Revenue Service's tax forms. None writes consistently clearly, and none gives you a concise view of planning your tax strategy. You'll do well to take this chapter as your best guide to strategy.

What to Do with Your Spare Cash

To most people, "investments" means stocks and bonds and mutual funds, but I've never met anyone who has made real money in stocks, bonds, or mutual funds unless he was rich in the first place. That doesn't mean you shouldn't own them, but you should recognize them for what they are: *supplements* to other investments such as real estate and small businesses that can *really* produce wealth. The stock market is a reasonably good place to achieve a decent return with no work, total liquidity (you can dump your stocks today and have cash tomorrow to buy a house), but some risk. If you've got $100,000, you may add $10,000 to $40,000 a year to it by careful stock market or mutual-fund investing. But if you've only got $10,000, you're probably talking about profits of $1,000 to $4,000 before taxes. That's hardly worth the bother — especially when you can get highly competitive interest rates from an intelligently selected bank account with much lower risk.

How the Stock Market Usually Works

I suspect my own experience in the stock market is typical. I've owned about twenty stocks and have made a net profit of $2,000. That means that if I'd never heard of the stock market, I'd be roughly as well-off financially as I am today.

In addition, I've also put about $3,000 in various stock options. They haven't produced any return at all. Last year, for example, my broker told me he had a hot idea. He had heard that ABC, the television network, was ripe for a takeover. The stock was selling at $65. For $600 I could buy options that would give me the right to purchase 2,000 shares at $75 until February 1985. If the takeover went through, the stock would probably go to $90, and I would make $12,000.

"Great," I said. I sent him a check for $600. And I started watching the financial pages more closely.

Nothing happened. The financial pages reported an occasional rumor that said what my broker had already told me, that ABC might be ripe for a takeover. But the stock price never approached $75.

The stock options expired on the third Thursday in February. Two weeks later, in March, I picked up the newspaper and read that ABC had been acquired by Capitol Cities Communications for $125 a share. If I had rolled my options over, I would have made over $40,000. This was my third "near-miss" in the options game.

There are two ways of looking at my experience. I could say that the option was a good investment and I just had some bad luck. But I think that's a Las Vegas gambler's way of thinking. Every losing poker player tells stories of near-misses. I consider options an investment structured to create near-misses and make money for brokers. Hundreds of thousands of people make their living watching the stock market. When my broker heard the report that ABC might be a takeover candidate, dozens of other market professionals were hearing it too. (ABC rose 10 points on the rumors.) Some bought the stock, others took advantage of the runup to sell ABC stock they already owned — and others sold options on shares they held at prices significantly higher than they could have received a few weeks before.

I had a reasonable chance of making $10,000 to $50,000 on my option, but dozens of events could have prevented my achieving any gain. To make money consistently in the stock market, you must be smarter or better informed than the thousands of other people betting against you. If I stayed away from options, I think I'm smart enough to make *some* money most of the time in the stock market. But I'd be deceiving myself if I expected to do much better than that — or to do nearly as well as I do in other investments.

If you like Las Vegas–style gambling, the options market gives you better odds than the roulette tables. But don't expect the stock market to make you rich. And if you don't want to bother with stocks, bonds, *or* mutual funds, I don't know any financial expert who feels that will keep you from getting ahead.

Managing Liquid Assets

Stocks, bonds, mutual funds, and bank accounts have one overwhelming advantage over other assets: they're liquid. Finding a buyer at the right price for a real estate investment can take six months or more. Your own business may be unsalable regardless of how profitable it is. But you can convert stocks, bonds, mutual-fund shares, or bank deposits to cash in one week or less. You can buy whenever you have some spare money and get out when you need to. You need not spend more than an hour a month managing them. Thus you can make money — a small amount of money — without much work.

As long as you have less than $20,000 or so in liquid assets, investing in stocks, mutual funds, and fixed-income securities is not too profitable. You'll want to find a nice, high-yielding parking lot for this cash, but it won't be generating more than a few thousand dollars a year in income.

When you have a reasonable nest egg, you may want to begin investing your spare cash a bit more aggressively. No-load and low-load mutual funds (discussed later in this chapter) are a reasonable vehicle. They're likely to do as well as anything else you can own unless you find an exceptionally good broker. You may even choose to use a couple of thousand dollars a year to speculate in options once you've accumulated $20,000 or so in cash.

Finally, some circumstances make investing in securities important even for people who don't yet possess a $20,000 nest egg. You can't easily put real estate into an Individual Retirement Account or a trust fund for your children. So it pays to understand a little bit about stocks, mutual funds, and other liquid assets.

Choosing a Parking Lot for Cash

Your first and easiest step is to choose a place to invest short-term excess cash. You can choose among more kinds of vehicles in this sector of investing than in any other. Bank money-market accounts, SuperNOW accounts, money-market mutual funds, and tax-exempt mutual funds are just the beginning. Some "experts" would have you believe you should also be dabbling in CDs, Treasury bills, and junk bonds. But in reality you can ignore most of these pieces of paper. Just find a place that gives a competitive return, put your money in it, and check every once in a while to be sure the return remains adequate.

First you must find out what a competitive rate *is* today. Any major newspaper can tell you the short-term rates big investors are getting. At least once a week, all large newspapers prominently display rates on securities with arcane names like "Treasury bills," "commercial paper," "repurchase agreements," etc. Don't worry about the meaning of these terms. Just look at rates for securities due in six months or less. (This includes "Treasury bills," "federal funds," and "commercial paper.") Usually the rates for all these securities are within a percent or so of each other. "Treasury bill" rates are for securities backed by the U.S. government. They involve essentially no risk. The most conservative bureaucrats in insurance companies and banks buy them when they have short-term cash to invest. "Commercial paper" is short-term debt of big companies.

At this point, ignore rates for any kind of "notes" or "bonds." These are longer-term securities.

The rates printed in your newspaper tell what's competitive today. The three-month Tresury bill rate makes a good benchmark. It jumps around a bit less than some other short-term rates, so it's a good gauge for what institutions should be paying you.

Your money should probably earn a bit more than the published rate on Treasury bills. When banks and other institutions borrow from large investors, they must pay more interest than the federal government because the bureaucratic investors who make most very-short-term investments perceive that investing in anything other than the federal government involves a little bit of risk. (Treasury bills also pay less because the interest is exempt from all state taxes.) Since banks must pay more than the U.S. Treasury to borrow money from big investors, they can afford to pay more than the U.S. Treasury to borrow from you. (And they sometimes prefer to borrow from small investors because small investors are less likely to jump somewhere else when rates change by a minuscule amount.)

To obtain a high rate of interest, you can consider four kinds of short-term investments: *bank money-market accounts, SuperNOW accounts, money-market mutual funds,* and *tax-exempt mutual funds.*

Bank Money-Market Accounts These accounts are supposed to pay a "money-market rate," which is Wall Street talk for a rate comparable to the rate on Treasury bills and such. They are generally good places to park money for a short time. You can usually write checks on these accounts, but only a limited number (usually three a month). And banks have an annoying habit of advertising money-market accounts with high rates, then cutting the rates substantially a few months later when thousands of people have deposited their money and most have stopped paying attention. So if you keep your money in a bank money-market account, you may want to compare the yield with Treasury bill rates every three to six months. On the other hand, keeping money in a bank money-market account may help build a relationship with the bank, and some banks give a free regular checking account to anyone who keeps a minimum balance in a money-market account.

SuperNOW Accounts Bank money-market accounts generally allow you to write only a few checks a month. SuperNOW accounts provide unlimited check-writing privileges in exchange for lower rates. Essentially, a SuperNOW account is a checking account that pays a reasonable rate of interest. NOW stands for "negotiable order of withdrawal," and technically the pieces of paper they give you when you open an account aren't checks but "negotiable orders of withdrawal." But they look like checks, smell like checks, and work like checks. Expect to get interest rates 1 to 1½ percent lower with a SuperNOW account than you get from a money-market account. Those lower rates buy you greater convenience. You probably should never keep more than $10,000 to $20,000 in any kind of NOW account, since moving $10,000 from a NOW account to a money-market account or money-market mutual fund will usually produce at least $100 a year in additional interest.

Money-Market Mutual Funds Mutual funds use your money to buy portfolios of securities. Then they pass along the income (or losses) they generate, after deducting money for operating expenses. Money-market mutual funds invest exclusively in short-term securities, so they consistently deliver money-market rates.

A money-market mutual fund typically yields slightly more than a money-market account at a bank. And money-market mutual funds (at least those from major investment houses) are among the most reliable investments in the world. While a bank executive can change the yield of a bank's money-market account on a whim, the yield of a money-market mutual fund is determined by the yield of the underlying securities. You need not worry that the fund will pull a fast one and cut rates after luring you in with lavish promises. Moreover, these funds typically allow you an unlimited number of checks, though you can only write checks of a minimum amount (usually $500).

Unfortunately, mutual-fund companies don't have offices around the corner and can't give you a loan when you need one. Keeping money in a money-market fund won't build the kind of relationship with your local bank that you'll want when you seek to borrow.

Tax-Exempt Mutual Funds   Some mutual funds invest in state and local government securities, which are exempt from federal — and some state and city — income taxes. Naturally these securities pay lower rates than taxable securities, but if your tax bracket is high enough, they may be worthwhile.

Unfortunately, there are two kinds of tax-exempt mutual funds, and the differences are important. *Tax-exempt money-market funds* work just like ordinary money-market funds except their dividends are tax-exempt. But states and cities don't issue too many short-term tax-exempt securities, and those that do exist pay low interest rates. So the largest share of tax-exempt funds are *tax-exempt bond funds*. These invest primarily in long-term securities, which usually offer more interest than short-term securities. But long-term securities have a drawback: unlike short-term securities, their prices often go down. They can hurt you every bit as much as poorly chosen or unlucky stocks.

Are Tax-Exempts for You?

People in a high tax bracket may want to consider short-term tax-exempt money-market funds as parking lots for their spare cash. You can often find tax-exempt mutual funds advertised in the Sunday financial section of your newspaper. (If you live in a state or city with an income tax, you'll of course want to look for funds whose income is exempt from your state and city's tax as well as from federal tax. These funds must be invested in your own state or city.

As a cash parking lot, however, be sure to consider only *tax-exempt money-market funds* — funds that invest in *short-term* securities. You may not find these prominently advertised in the newspaper. The fund companies usually find the higher-interest *bond* funds easier to sell. (The risks are listed deep in the prospectuses.) Be sure to check the maturity on the paper to determine the value of this investment.

If you find a tax-exempt money-market fund that appears to be appropriate to your needs, compare its yield with the *after-tax* yield of Treasury bills or another short-term taxable investment. Multiply:

the yield of Treasury bills × (1 − your total tax bracket)

That will give you the after-tax yield of a Treasury bill. If that after-tax yield is significantly less than the yield of a short-term tax-exempt money-market fund, the tax-exempt fund may be a good deal for you.

If you can't find a short-term fund that exempts you from the taxes of your state or city, you may want to consider a tax-exempt fund that invests in long-term bonds for a portion of your securities portfolio. But be sure to compare the yield of the tax-exempt bond fund with the after-tax yield of a *long-term* taxable investment such as a mutual fund that invests in long-term corporate bonds. And remember that any long-term fixed-income investment involves great risks. (See "Long-term 'Fixed-Income' Investments," below.) Never make any investment that involves long-term fixed-income securities unless you think long-term interest rates are *declining*. And never put more than, say, 25 percent of your cash into it.

Finally, if you can't readily find a tax-exempt fund that serves your needs, don't waste time worrying. If you've got, say, $20,000 in spare cash, the after-tax difference between investing in a taxable money-market account and investing in a tax-free fund won't exceed a few hundred dollars a year.

Choosing a Bank Account or a Money-Market Mutual Fund

There are more powerful ways to shelter income, as we showed in chapter 10, so you may have no interest in tax-free securities. That will make life much easier.

If you're not interested in tax sheltering, chances are these days that you can walk into your nearest bank and find a perfectly acceptable place to invest spare cash. The days when banks couldn't or wouldn't pay rates competitive with money-market mutual funds are largely gone. If the money-market account at your local bank pays as much as the current Treasury bill rate, it's a good place to put your money. If you find a money-market account's minimums or its limitations on check writing difficult to cope with, you can keep all or a large fraction of your spare cash in a NOW account.

And if you're annoyed about the way banks advertise big yields and then cut them below the market rate when no one is looking, you can put your money in a money-market mutual fund. But then you'll have to maintain a checking account separately at a bank.

I recommend a money-market account at a bank you trust.

Long-term "Fixed-Income" Investments

While looking at cash parking lots, you may have been tempted by the higher yields that long-term bonds pay. After all, long-term bonds and shares in the mutual funds that invest in them *can* be sold and turned quickly into cash, so you can get higher yields from them with little or no apparent sacrifice in liquidity.

The problem is that when interest rates rise, the price of bonds goes down — sometimes dramatically. Suppose the U.S. Treasury issues a $1,000, 10 percent bond. It will pay $100 a year in interest. Now suppose interest rates rise to 12 percent. Investors looking to buy bonds can now get $100 a year in interest from new bonds that cost them only $833, so they won't buy old Treasury bonds for much more than that. (If you're not quick with math, 12 percent of $833 is $100.) The value of the old $1,000 bond will have declined sharply.

The reverse can happen when interest rates fall: long-term-bond prices can rise. Big professional investors may make a lot of money in bonds if the United States gets its budget deficit under control and long-term rates fall, but *you* probably can't make real money on this kind of swing unless you have hundreds of thousands of dollars to invest or unless you spend quite a bit of time investigating bonds. The long-term-bond market — and mutual funds investing in it — is not a place to invest spare cash casually.

Long-term fixed-income investments do have appropriate places in portfolios — in some people's IRAs or trust accounts for their children's college educations, for example, where they may want steady, consistent accumulation. But don't be tempted to store ordinary spare cash in these investments.

Thinking About the Stock Market?

Competition in the stock market is far more sophisticated than you'll find almost anywhere else in business. When you go to a broker to buy a stock, the broker and the stock exchange must match your order with the order of someone else who has decided to sell. Whenever you buy, you're betting that you know where the stock's price is going better than the guy who sold to you.

But on the average, stocks *do* make money. The stock market averages have outperformed bank accounts in most years since World War II. In the ten-year period from early 1975 through early 1985 — a mediocre period for the stock market — the stocks in Standard & Poor's 500 stock index produced average returns of 14.6 percent a year. You could beat that by a big margin in real estate, but you couldn't equal it if you kept your money in bank accounts. Moreover, from the tax man's point of view, much of your stock market profit would be long-term capital gains and most of your losses should be short-term capital losses (see chapter 10), so you should pay far less tax than you would on bank-account interest. Thus you may want to put some of your cash in stocks or mutual funds.

As your businesses start generating cash flow, the stock market will become very tempting. Opportunities to invest on your own — properties to buy cheaply or small businesses to invest in — won't show up at the rate you'd need to keep your funds fully invested. Once you've got a bundle of cash, stock market investing makes sense.

The Simple Strategy: Mutual Funds

Picking stocks, unfortunately, is tough. In many — perhaps most — years, the average "professionally managed" portfolio does worse than such market averages as the Standard & Poor's 500 stock index. Thus you shouldn't assume that you or any broker will consistently pick stocks that beat the market. You may be lucky in picking stocks, or you may be lucky in finding a broker who knows how to pick stocks, but don't count on it. And brokers can take as much as 8 percent of your money when you initially invest and more later in fees for maintaining your account.

A simple and relatively safe way to invest in stocks is to put money in a "no-load" or possibly a "low-load" mutual fund. Most mutual-fund portfolios achieve no better returns than any other "professionally managed" portfolios, but at least you need not pay any fee to buy or sell shares in the no-load variety. A few funds do seem to do better than the averages for years at a time (though when they are "discovered" by the general public, their character may change). And you can easily switch among various kinds of funds as conditions change in the market.

"No-load" funds are mutual funds that make no sales or redemption charges. Their managers make their money and pay their expenses by deducting a small amount from the fund's net asset value every year, usually about 0.6 percent. "Load" funds charge a fee of up to 8 percent of your money when you buy and sometimes another fee when you sell. They also charge roughly the same annual management fees that no-load funds charge. The difference between the two is in the way they're marketed: load funds use their loads to pay professional salesmen, while no-load funds basically wait for you to come to them.

No-load funds hire no professional salesmen. In fact, even finding information on a selection of no-load funds can be a problem. The no-load funds do sometimes buy small ads in newspapers. Try to get a copy of the issue of *Barron's* that contains its most recent quarterly mutual-fund performance survey. It will give you comparisons of performance, and it will also contain ads from a variety of no-load funds.

The Fidelity Group of Boston, which is the nation's largest mutual-fund company, recently invented the "low-load" fund by placing small sales charges — generally 3 percent — on some of its most attractive funds. Two large mutual-fund groups, Fidelity and the Vanguard Group of Valley Forge, Pennsylvania, manage to place some of their funds on most lists of top performers.

Any mutual-fund company will be delighted to send you a prospectus — a legal document that tells about the fund and contains performance statistics and (usually if the performance is good) charts. Seek a fund whose performance record has been superior over the past one, five, ten, and fifteen years to that of the Standard & Poor's 500 stock index. (Comparisons with the Dow Jones Industrial Averages are generally useless. The Dow consists of thirty leading manufacturing companies, and it doesn't really represent the breadth of the market.)

Then ask whether the strategy that has worked so well for this fund so far may not perhaps be exhausted. (Natural resource–oriented funds did well in the early seventies, but faded after that, for example.) If the long-term performance is good and the strategy still seems sound, go ahead and invest.

Try to choose funds that will let you get your money out by telephone. You simply call an 800 number and tell them to send you your money, and they do it. (You can also have money wired to your bank account.)

Interest Rates, Fund Families, and Switching

Many funds belong to "families," and you can switch among them with a phone call to an 800 telephone number. This is particularly useful when interest rates rise.

Interest-rate increases usually cause the stock market to stagnate or decline. Many investors sell their stocks and move to high-interest money-market investments.

It's a good idea to be among the first to get out of the market when rates rise. If the rates offered in the money market seem overwhelmingly tempting, don't resist.

The fund families all include money-market funds, so you can switch your investment into the money market in hours without a commission charge.

A Choosier Strategy

If you want to pick your own stocks, Jeff Devers, vice-president for new-product development for Oppenheimer and Company,

suggests a conservative strategy based on options. Devers agrees
that ordinary young investors don't *need* to invest in stocks, options, *or* mutual funds. He points out that the dangers of stock
market (or mutual-fund) investing are always considerable. "Maybe
one year out of five stocks go down 20 percent or more," says
Devers. "If that year happens to be your first year in the market,
it'll be five more years till you're ahead of where you would have
been if you had stayed in the bank. That's just not a good risk to
take with cash that you're investing between other deals."

Instead of a mutual-fund or stock strategy, Devers suggests banking all but, say, 5 to 10 percent of your funds, and using the 5 to
10 percent to buy options. Options are cheap, Devers argues, and
this means you can take the interest your money is earning in the
bank, invest it in options, and have a good shot at the same profits
you'd earn if you put half or more of your money in risky stocks.
And at the same time, your principal in the bank remains un-
touched. You have *absolutely no risk of loss* of the principal.

It can work. After all, the options that *almost* made me $50 a
share on ABC only cost me 30 cents each. But my experience with
options says: be prepared for disappointment.

And whatever you do in the stock market, don't count on it as
your major investment vehicle. It won't make your fortune.

Accumulating Funds for the Far Future

Some of the planning and tax maneuvers I mentioned in the last
chapter create pools of money that need to be invested quite differently from your main collection of cash. You may want to put
some of your Individual Retirement Account and children's trust-
fund money in long-term fixed-income investments when you
wouldn't consider them for the cash that's simply waiting to be
reinvested in another business deal. Moreover, the tax advantages
of stock and mutual-fund investing become irrelevant when your
investment is already tax-sheltered.

Generally, you build IRAs and trust funds for specific, well-
defined goals. You want to accumulate $1 million for your retire-
ment or $100,000 for your kids' education. If you use an IRA or
a trust fund to buy a fixed-income security to hold till it matures,
you know exactly what you are getting. Because you know its value
at maturity, you know roughly how close it brings you to your
goals. (You don't know *exactly* how close it brings you, because

you *don't* know how much inflation will reduce the value of those dollars.)

Many people simply invest their IRAs and children's trust funds in money-market accounts, but long-term certificates of deposit or other securities may produce a higher rate that's guaranteed for as long as ten years. One option especially worthwhile for these accounts is a *zero-coupon* certificate of deposit or bond. Most long-term securities pay interest semiannually or at least every year. Managing that income within an IRA or trust account can be a pain. But a zero-coupon security pays a lump sum at the end of a specified period. You simply pay $1,000 in return for the promise that you'll receive several times your money some years from now.

Investment Houses: Which Are Right for You?

If you know *what* you want to do with your money, you're three-quarters of the way to deciding *what investment house* or houses you want to use. You have four kinds to choose from: *banks, mutual-fund companies, discount brokerage houses,* and *full-service brokerage houses.*

Banks Banks claim to be able to meet all your financial needs. They can provide money-market accounts, long-term CDs, Individual Retirement Accounts, and trust accounts for your children. Some now seek to sell a variety of other products as well.

When you first start out on your own, you don't need any other investment house besides a bank, but you'll eventually want to go beyond a bank. If you set up an Individual Retirement Account, for example, think twice before doing it through a bank. It's difficult to move an IRA out of a bank if the bank reduces its certificate-of-deposit rates. And mutual funds have performed significantly better than any product widely offered by banks today.

Everything in the banking business is changing, albeit slowly. Today some banks want to sell you stocks and mutual funds. Generally they do this through some sort of deal with an existing discount broker or mutual-fund company.

If the broker or mutual-fund company is good, the deal may be good, but generally I'd avoid buying any investments more complex than a certificate of deposit from a bank unless your banker can explain exactly what their arrangement is. Use your bank for ordinary deposits and loans, but go elsewhere if you seek more exotic investments.

Mutual-Fund Companies As indicated earlier, mutual-fund companies let you dabble in the markets without paying large commissions. Try to choose a no-load mutual fund whose parent company will let you redeem shares or switch into other funds by telephone.

Discount Brokerage Houses Originally, discount brokers were simply order takers for big, sophisticated investors. To a large extent that's still their character, but the leading discount brokers do try to provide some information to help people like us make investment decisions.

If you want to become seriously involved with the markets, you definitely need an account with a discount broker. When you know what you want to buy or sell, the discount broker will always execute the transaction for you more cheaply than an ordinary "full-service" broker. And the "service" you get from a "full-service" broker too often consists simply of efforts to sell you something that will generate brokerage commissions.

Ideally, when you call a discount broker you should know exactly what you want to buy or sell. But if you know only approximately what you want to buy, the discount broker is still worth a call. If, for example, you know you want a zero-coupon bond certificate of deposit that will mature in fifteen years (say, for a trust account that will put your kids through college), but you don't yet know who issues such certificates, a discount brokerage house may be able to tell you.

Full-Service Brokerage Houses Most well-known brokerage houses, including all those that advertise most heavily, are "full-service" brokerage houses. Of course, they charge higher commissions than the discounters.

Unfortunately, most full-service brokers simply don't make much money for their clients. There's absolutely no evidence that the stocks that brokers recommend perform any better on average than stocks that brokers don't recommend. Thus when full-commission brokers call you, you have no more guarantee that you're going to get beneficial "service" than when you get a call from a vacuum-cleaner or life-insurance salesman.

However, if you insist on investing in the stock market, full-service brokers *do* have their place, especially if you do not have the time or inclination to follow the market yourself. And full-service brokers can give you some types of advice that you'll never get from a bank, a mutual-fund company, or a discount broker. If you want to do something fancy with your IRA and you don't know exactly how, ask around and see if a friend can recommend a good broker.

Unfortunately, however, anyone with less than $100,000 to invest in the markets really can't generate enough commissions to make himself a worthwhile client for a first-rate full-service broker. So don't expect superb advice *or* service. And remember that the broker gets paid by how much trading you do, not by how much money you make. Consider his recommendations *very* skeptically.

Fancy Deals

I should add one special word of caution. Probably the *least* reliable investment ideas you can get from *any* investment broker are ideas that look *most* like the one I recommended in chapters 4 through 9. I like small business and real estate deals. That should be clear from the entire first portion of this book. But there's nothing inherently good about small business and real estate deals. They can mean disaster when they're sold by high-overhead brokerage houses.

You can make money on your own in small businesses and real estate because you'll be using your own creativity to do things that might not get done without you. But when a big brokerage firm packages a real estate deal or promotes a small business, it's contributing the creativity that you should be providing — and to turn a profit, it must take a markup that includes a lot of overhead.

Always remember: You get rich when you use your own creativity and management ability to create *value*. You can't get rich just by giving money to a stockbroker. And you're especially unlikely to get rich by giving money to a stockbroker for the kinds of investments you should be creating on your own.

Managing Well

Richard is a clergyman in New York City. His father was a salesman for Sears, Roebuck, his mother a stay-at-home housewife. Eight years ago, when he was in his midthirties, he had less than $500 in cash and no investments.

Today Richard owns some $500,000 worth of property. He has never been on "the fast track"; he has always remained true to his ideals; he has never devoted more than a few hours a week to making money; he's done nothing that required special skills; and he has succeeded brilliantly.

Richard's experience and the experiences of some other people I've met show that a person like *you* can achieve your goals and build some wealth. Several have impressed me particularly as examples of how ordinary people can get their finances and their entire economic lives in order, and I want to introduce them in this chapter.

"Wise as Serpents, Harmless as Doves"

Richard had no role model when he first got into real estate. But part of his motivation was theological. "In the New Testament, Jesus says, 'Be wise as serpents and harmless as doves.' If I see an opportunity where I can manipulate the system in a beneficial way, I should take advantage of it. I believe that it is better to get in and play the game ethically than abstain and leave it to people who will be exploitative.

"I'm also in real estate for personal reasons. I want to secure the futures of my children. Neither my wife nor I had much security growing up. I also give a lot of money to charity." (Richard's tax return showed that he had given away about 20 percent of his taxable income last year.)

Richard had believed in home ownership from childhood, but as he approached his thirty-fifth birthday, he realized he was making no progress toward accumulating a down payment. When he found a coop apartment selling for only $20,000 on Manhattan's Upper West Side, he borrowed $5,000 from a friend and went to a banker to apply for a loan. Before visiting the banker, he deposited the $5,000 in a savings account so that a credit check would show he had some assets. He got the loan and bought the place.

Richard lived in the apartment for two years and sold it for $42,000. The friend who had lent him $5,000 said he'd be just as happy to continue receiving interest from Richard as to get his $5,000 back, so Richard had $27,000 in his bank account after repaying the mortgage.

Next Richard bought a $45,000 loft — a space formerly used for manufacturing — in the Chelsea section of Manhattan. He put $10,000 down, took out a mortgage for the rest, and planned to use the rest of his money — and a lot of sweat — to fix the place up. Fixing up turned out to require not only most of his cash but also a good deal of debt he ran up on credit cards. But he managed to split the loft into one 3,000-square-foot apartment for his family and one 2,000-square-foot apartment that he rented out. He was ready for a tenant after six weeks of work during a summer vacation.

Richard and two partners then bought two more floors in the same building. Richard had used most of his bank and credit card borrowing capacity, so he asked his father to invest $12,000. Richard was taking a significant share of his father's life savings, but by now he could confidently promise that he would return double the amount "borrowed." The three partners bought the two floors for $112,000, fixed them up, and sold them for $287,000. Richard paid his father $24,000 and was left with a $46,000 share of the profits.

The next year Richard sold the 2,000-square-foot apartment he had created on the floor where he lived. He got $125,000. He had now been devoting a few hours a week to real estate for almost five years, and he had taken out $200,000 cash. He used the money from the apartment sale to buy a house in Maine.

Two years later he bought an old schoolhouse in Beacon, New York, where he is creating seven condominiums. Richard and his wife expect the condos will sell for more than $600,000 and they'll get $125,00 in profits.

Richard says he has enjoyed every deal but the most recent, which has taken a lot of time to put together. Until this year he rarely spent more than five hours a week on real estate, and it made no dent in the fifty to sixty hours a week he was putting into his ministry. But creating the condominium project has meant driving regularly to Beacon, an hour and a half north of New York City. Otherwise, Richard is happy with his part-time career. He has had little trouble making money, although he has avoided being a landlord. "I tend to get personally involved with people, and if I had to be a landlord, I'm afraid I would wind up getting nasty," he says. In fact, Richard avoids almost everything that gives people ethical qualms about real estate investing. He doesn't evict people, and he doesn't gentrify neighborhoods. He buys vacant buildings, improves them, and sells them.

Richard has achieved financial independence by doing good, and has done it in a way that most other people could do as well.

Rick Pallack: A Fortune in His Own Business

When I was in high school, one friend of mine was famous for knowing how to dress: Rick Pallack. Rick's life shows that although getting started in business can be a grind, most people can do it by concentrating on what they know. Rick took what he knew and made the most of it.

He started learning about clothing before the age of ten. His father was a manufacturers' representative who sold clothes to stores on commission. Rick liked visiting stores.

Young Rick soon broke into the business himself by making cuff links his father sold to clients. But while Rick's products sold, his father did poorly. Rick's parents were divorced, and he and his mother wound up living on her earnings as a bookkeeper and what Rick could make working in clothing stores. Thus Rick was highly motivated to establish his own business. By the time we were juniors in high school, Rick had a thriving trade: he was selling shirts and pants from the trunk of a car he'd bought. Rick really knew how to put together an outfit.

After high school, Rick rented a large apartment and began using it as a store. He had been saving business cards of customers at fancy stores where he had worked as a salesman. He focused on providing totally coordinated outfits for people, especially in the entertainment and music businesses, who lacked both the time and the desire to pick out their own clothes. He promoted the store with mailings and phone calls, and did $1 million a year in business from the apartment in 1980. After that it was an easy step to launching a conventional store.

Today "Rick Pallack" is the leading high-fashion, off-price men's store in the Los Angeles area. Pallack knows how to promote himself. He's done the men's wardrobes for *Dynasty, Falcon Crest,* and *Days of Our Lives.* He's sold street clothes to Michael Jackson and family, Sugar Ray Leonard, and Billy Dee Williams.

But Pallack insists that he isn't necessarily loaded with charisma. He just learned to do something well and stuck with it. "If I'd been raised around supermarkets I'd probably own a chain of supermarkets today," he says. The key was getting practical experience and then stepping out as an entrepreneur. "If I didn't work in a store as a kid, I'd just have gone to school like everyone else. I wouldn't have gotten the business sense, and I don't know where I'd be."

At the same time, Pallack points out that most people have practical experience in *something.* By sticking with that something, motivated people can build a business like Pallack's.

Gene Murrow: A Prosperous Teacher

In high school I also had a math teacher, Gene Murrow. I could tell Mr. Murrow liked to teach. He taught the advanced math classes in school and stayed after school to play at proving theorems with kids and coach the math team. He and his students built a computer — a daring and unusual achievement in 1975. They took it to several trade shows and even sold a few to businesses.

Mr. Murrow loved teaching, but his goals went beyond teaching. He wanted to live creatively and solve new problems. Moreover, he wanted to participate in the excitement rolling through the computer business in those days. Yet he also didn't want to leave teaching, his first passion.

"I thought about my talents and talked them over with a student's father, who was a venture capitalist," Murrow recalls. "What I really liked doing was teaching, and what people wanted me to do was teach them about computers. I thought about where I could teach them best, and I realized that what was needed was a computer store. So I decided to set one up."

Gene was one of the inventors of the personal-computer store. In 1975 most people hadn't even realized the world would *need* special stores to teach people how to use computers. Gene sold his house and moved to an apartment to raise $60,000 for the business, and the venture capitalist he had met raised an additional $50,000.

Gene had never done any selling in his life, but the venture capitalist gave him good advice. It's relatively easy to hire salesmen and pay their wages if you have something valuable to sell, the friend pointed out. Gene hired young people, mostly people with some experience selling either in stores or to businesses. None knew much about computers, but Gene could teach the salesmen as well as his customers.

The business took off like a rocket. After a couple of years, Xerox put in $250,000 for 18 percent of the business. Murrow sold his share of the business a few years later and moved back East, taking out a big profit.

Then, at a time when industry pundits were declaring that the independent computer retailer could never survive, he found a new way to make money teaching. He now runs a business that sells and teaches people how to use computers in a narrow and poorly served field: he is one of the leading computer vendors to the construction industry in New York State. He's a wealthy, happy man.

Obviously, many teachers can't become millionaires by teaching, but Murrow's success shows that opportunities do exist to combine wealth even with passions like teaching. Most people's deepest desires *can* earn them a good living. They just need to find out how their desires relate to what people want and need to buy.

Eli Portnoy: A Good Business without Abandoning a Career

Most people don't even need to quit their current jobs to build a business. Eli Portnoy did it without taking more than a few hours a week — and without investing more than $100 in capital.

Eli's part-time career began when a friend arrived for a tennis match one day in what appeared to be an all-silver sweatsuit. Eli asked about it and learned that it was a one-piece oversuit that technicians wore over their street clothes when handling dangerous materials. It was designed to be disposable — people usually threw out a suit every day after wearing it. But it was made of a petroleum-based DuPont material called Tyvec, and it was strong and durable. Eli thought it was neat and would make great play clothes.

Eli got in touch with the manufacturer and learned that the suits cost only $1.85 at wholesale. He bought twenty for less than $50. He named the suits "Pogo jumpsuits," sewed a label of his own into them, and offered them for sale to friends and acquaintances for $11.95 each. All he ever had to invest in the business was $50 for suits and labels.

Eli's friends immediately liked the suits as well as he had. With the profits from the initial sales, Eli went back to the manufacturer for several more orders of twenty, forty, or sixty suits. Soon he had made several thousand dollars, and he had enough money to hire a family friend to do a photo for a small magazine ad. He ran it in *Los Angeles* and *New York* magazines. The ads cost $2,000 each and produced $8,000 in orders for a profit of about $3,000. Eli also spent weekends for a summer selling the jumpsuits and other silvery items he had the industrial supplier make up, at a small store his parents owned in Amagansett, Long Island. After half a year in the business, total sales were some 2,500 garments for $30,000.

Macy's and Bloomingdale's were interested in the product, but Eli faced a problem. The industrial supplier had a nice, safe business producing a few thousand jumpsuits a month for industrial users. He wouldn't expand production to meet the demands of the fashion trade — whose orders might disappear in a few months. To continue building his business, Eli would have to quit his regular job and work full-time on Pogo, learning to deal with traditional garment-industry suppliers. If he wouldn't do that, he would have to take his profits and give up the business. (He couldn't expect to continue as a hobby for long because others in the industry would see the opportunities in Tyvec and come out with better-tailored versions at better prices.)

Eli decided to close the business. He cleared $18,000 for six months' part-time work. Moreover, he learned that he really *can* sense what people will want to buy. Now he's starting a new part-time business, importing handmade glass items from Italy. "Just having a job is not enough for me. I'm doing well, but I've got an entrepreneurial spirit that compels me to explore any opportunity. I want to live comfortably and fulfill this desire," he says.

Eli's experience shows you can start a business in your spare time — if you can find the right idea.

Chris Whittle: A Role Model of My Own

Personally, I look at Chris Whittle, the chairman of the 13–30 Corporation and of *Esquire* magazine, as a role model. Whittle and friends set out in college to build a communications company, and that's what I'd like to do someday, too.

As mentioned in chapter 1, Whittle and buddies at the University of Tennessee at Knoxville started with a very small business when they were students around 1970. They proved they could make money at it, then expanded it into a major corporation. They simply kept taking on bigger and more worthwhile challenges as they learned their business better.

Whittle notes that he and his friends could never have done what they did if they hadn't pulled together a partnership with diverse skills from among the students at the University of Tennessee. Phillip Moffitt, now president of 13–30 Corp. and publisher and editor-in-chief of *Esquire,* was the concept guy: he had good ideas and the ability to think them through. Chris was the conceptual marketing man — a talker and charmer and salesman. An older friend, David White, was a stable, careful thinker. He became chairman of the board and handled the finance issues. (White "retired" from 13–30 in his midthirites with a substantial sum and now spends his time investing in new companies and doing whatever else he wants.) The partnership also involved several other friends. The partners were mainly the sons of small-town Tennessee professionals.

The group launched *Knoxville in a Nutshell* by selling ads to dry cleaners, restaurants, and movie houses. Then they set out to take the business national, placing editions of the magazine *Nutshell* on every major college campus. They also sought to produce special magazines dedicated to individual clients' needs.

It was tough work. *Nutshell* couldn't make it as a national magazine without the support of national advertisers. But college kids in the early seventies were telling everyone that they had no interest in material possessions — and that meant they had no interest in buying advertisers' goods. The local restaurants in Knoxville had known that kids had money to spend and were spending it. National advertisers didn't believe it. (A company that had tried to convince them of the same general idea a few years earlier, National Student Marketing, had become a Wall Street darling until investors discovered that creative accounting produced all its profits. The New York media didn't want to be burned again.)

Within two years after deciding to take Nutshell national, 13–30 Corp. had accumulated $1 million in liabilities. As Whittle puts it, "We were in so deep we didn't have much choice but to stay in. We saw early signs of interest, but advertisers mostly took a wait-and-see approach."

But the business slowly grew. Advertisers who bought ads in *Nutshell* found it was a good medium. It became a recognized source of information around many major campuses. And a few major clients, such as Nissan Motors, signed for specialized magazines. Nissan's magazine is about traveling in America. Advertisers realized that *Nutshell* knew how to reach its audience, and they began to buy ads almost automatically. The company is now an unqualified success. Their revenues doubled every two years during the past eight years.

When 13–30 bought *Esquire* magazine in 1979, no one in New York believed in Whittle and Moffitt. *Esquire* had lost millions of dollars for two well-established publishing companies, and was generally considered a hopeless investment. "I've never heard of these people," *Esquire* National Editor Richard Reeves said of Whittle and Moffitt, who at the time were thirty-one and thirty-two years old. "They could have landed from Mars."

Even Whittle and Moffitt's greatest admirers would have acknowledged that *Nutshell* couldn't compare with the greatest achievements of a publication that had once been a showcase for Ernest Hemingway and F. Scott Fitzgerald. But Whittle, Moffitt, and others in the 13–30 organization had learned publishing at the grass roots. They knew who they needed to please to make a publication successful. And they deeply believed, even in the cynical 1970s, that there was a market for the idea that had launched *Esquire* in the 1930s: a magazine about "Man at His Best."

Esquire became one of the greatest turnaround stories in the magazine business. It's now solidly profitable and genuinely worthwhile.

What's the Lesson of These People?

Some of these people have based their businesses on skills or contacts you probably don't possess. Eli Portnoy, for example, had some sense of how people sell fashion products because his mother runs an art gallery. Everyone in this chapter built a business based on something they had "insider" knowledge about. Whittle knew about the youth market, Pallack knew clothes.

Think about what expertise you have. *You* have skills and contacts that Pallack, Portnoy, and Whittle didn't possess. Accomplishing *your* goals may not make you as financially independent as they are, and may involve even more hard work, but if you think your goal out clearly and plan for success, you can accumulate wealth and, if you want, build a business by concentrating on what you know. You can build a business that lets you do what you want to do. And (though of course your options will be more limited) you can even build a business without quitting or neglecting your current job.

But even if this is not enough for you, almost anyone can do what Richard did; making a fortune by managing buildings in his spare time. And most people can produce something like the successes of the others in this chapter — in fact, something like the successes of others I've mentioned thoughout this book — if they decide what they want to do, develop a clear idea, and decide they're willing to pay the price that may be required to get a business started.

This is how you can achieve your goals in life.

Can You REALLY Do It?

In trying to educate myself about money and then later in preparing to write about it, I must have read twenty different personal-finance books. None — except perhaps for a couple of real estate books listed in Appendix B — left me convinced that I could actually follow their advice and get ahead.

Some books advise you to accumulate $100 a week for thirty years so you'll have $40,000,000 including compound interest when you retire. Others provide little substantive advice at all — only a collection of cute stories that leave you just as puzzled as ever about your financial future.

Many of these books left me with the distinct impression that their authors got rich from book and newsletter royalties, not from following the strategies they recommended. Are these people *really* willing to sacrifice for thirty years to make *themselves* comfortable?

If you approach how-to books as skeptically as I do, you've already spent some time wondering about whether the ideas in *this* book are as good as I claim. If you've read this far, you're at least partially convinced that I know what I'm talking about. You're persuaded that I'm offering advice better than most other personal-finance books. But you've no doubt gotten this far in other how-to books and realized a few months later that they hadn't changed your life at all.

Right now you should be thinking about whether the ideas in this book are good enough to justify the actions you'll have to take to put them into practice. Can you really invest and build businesses to achieve your goals in life? Or, if your goals aren't yet well-defined, can you really invest and manage money to build the wealth you'll want in the future?

You can. You can build wealth or reach any other goal using the strategies in this book. And you should. I don't know whether your current goals are the right goals for you, but I do know that you'll need to learn to manage resources well in order to reach any worthwhile goal. And most people who are wealthy today have used the same techniques I've outlined in this book to create their fortunes.

In this chapter I want to answer some of the fears that may be lurking in your mind. Then I'll give you a push toward exercising the little bit of self-discipline necessary to succeed. Most often you fail to learn "how to" from a how-to book because its authors have nothing worthwhile to say. But sometimes you probably fail to learn because you fail to take the advice you meant to follow. I hope that won't happen after you read this book.

I'm Too Busy to Invest"

Probably the most common excuse for mismanaging finances today is "I'm too busy." And sometimes when people claim they're "too busy," there's truth in the assertion. Some people really *are* too busy "making a living" to produce the kind of money they could earn by investing independently. But that doesn't mean they should ignore their finances. It just means they need special strategies.

If you're a medical intern or a research scientist or an investment banker working a sixty-five-hour week, you obviously won't be able to spend the time on your own affairs that people in other professions can. The benefits of your job must make up for the limited chance you'll have to develop your life independently.

But that *isn't* an excuse for neglecting independent goals completely. You have to live somewhere; why not buy a place whose value you can increase? Finding one may take only a few days, and you can spread those days out over six months if necessary. You need not invest any time in improving a place once you've bought it — you can hire people to clean and paint and still come out ahead by tens of thousands of dollars. (I made $78,000 that way, and many other people have done just as well.)

If you already own a place, why not flip it — move to another place more convenient to your job? The time you spend flipping can be recovered in a few months by reduced commuting time. You can liberate tens of thousands of dollars and position yourself for even greater capital gains ahead with only a few days' work.

If you think you don't have time to invest, you probably won't be starting a business of your own. But the job that demands so many hours of your time may also put you in touch with creative people who will be starting businesses of *their* own. It takes none of your time at all to listen for investment opportunities among your friends and business associates. Keeping up with their ideas and struggles will even give you a better understanding of the real world that can benefit you in your main job.

So if you think you don't have time to invest, don't give up investing. Just invest in things that require little time.

"I Still Don't Think I Have Money to Invest"

Are you still doubting that you can afford to invest? Maybe some people can't start investing immediately — people who have just lost a job, or who have not accumulated any savings, perhaps. But I believe anyone can begin investing in six months to a year, except possibly during periods when interest rates are exceptionally high. If you're the sort of person who saves, you may want to wait till you have $6,000 or $10,000 accumulated. But if you're not, you're better off getting started with a leveraged investment program as soon as possible. With a couple thousand dollars, established credit, and intelligent use of other people's money, most people can buy homes for themselves. And anyone who has owned a well-chosen home for more than a year has equity that can serve as the basis for future investments.

If you have trouble figuring out how a person with your balance sheet can get started making money, think again about these sources:

- Have you added up your borrowing power? Have you considered:
  1. loans from your family,
  2. loans from your company,
  3. loans from any credit union you may have rights at,
  4. credit card loans, and
  5. personal loans you'd qualify for at a bank?
- Have you considered buying a home or a rental property with

a second mortgage from the seller? How about financing for a new home or condominium from a builder?

- Have you considered getting together with a friend to buy a home or other property?
- If you already own a home, do you know how much it's really worth today? Have you looked at the many opportunities to borrow against your property?

There's one other category of people who may think they haven't any money to invest: the as-yet-unsuccessful entrepreneur. If you're starting a business and there's no money coming in, then you're "investing" in the business right now. If the business is a couple of years old and there's *still* no money coming in, then you're *still* investing. But it's time you considered whether you're investing as wisely as possible.

Does it still make sense to continue in this business? If it's your life's dream, you probably won't want to give it up. (One guy I know studied wine-making for three years and now runs a winery that's showing just the faintest glimmers of profitability.) But shouldn't you be investing some of your time in something a bit less risky?

Most businesses give you flexibility with your time and contacts in the business world. If your business involves wholesaling something, should you find some other product — perhaps produced by a foreign potential competitor — you can sell along with your own? Or should you search for a real estate investment? If you've developed a good relationship with an insurance man, a real estate professional, or a banker, he may be able to point you toward opportunities that require management skills, not cash.

"Investing Would Be Too Risky for Me Now"

When people say they can't afford to invest, they usually don't mean they absolutely *couldn't* buy a property now. They're usually saying that buying would be too risky. They'd have to take out loans, and that makes them nervous. What would happen if the value of the property went down?

Some kinds of good investments *are* risky. Perhaps it wouldn't be wise for you to invest in a new start-up computer company yet. And if you don't buy carefully, you *can* wind up over your head even in real estate. But it isn't risky to invest in a good home of your own if you seek out *value*. It's risky *not* to invest in one.

Someday you may lose your job, get divorced, or want to raise children. If you buy a home or rental property, you're almost certain to build up equity. If you haven't bought one, any increase in the size of your family or any misfortune that may befall you can create *real* trouble for you. If you think investing is risky, talk to someone who is trying to raise young children or cope with a divorce *without* the cushion of owning an asset.

"I'm Afraid I'd Mess Things Up"

Do you still doubt you have the skill to make money investing on your own? You're not alone, but you're probably underestimating yourself.

Most people who think they can't invest come from families who never invested creatively. They may have received warnings as children about the dangers of debt and risk. They're vaguely aware that they're smarter than half the rich people in the world. Yet they somehow believe they can't do what made the rich people rich.

Two elements contribute to this lack of self-confidence:

• a genuine recognition of significant weaknesses, and
• simple, irrational fear.

Real weaknesses are easiest to deal with. Just write down what you think you can't do well. Try "brainstorming" about your weaknesses in the same way I suggested you brainstorm about goals in chapter 2: quickly list everything you think you may not be good at. Then go back and cross off the fears that are probably unfounded. When you've listed your weaknesses, recognize that you must either be very careful about how you handle activities where you're weak, or arrange to let others handle those jobs.

Many people, for instance, find they are easily pushed into things and poor at selling anything to others. These are serious weaknesses. But they need not destroy your economic life.

The lack of salesmanship may be relatively easy to cope with. Unless you dream of launching a peculiar, idiosyncratic business, you can arrange much of your business life so others do your selling for you. For example, you'll probably want to hire a real estate broker when you sell your real estate. Just be sure to interview several brokers before hiring one and think carefully about who will do the best job for you.

Being easily pushed into things is the greatest danger, especially if you don't have friends who will push you into the *right* things. Seek a trusted friend's advice when you invest. Be especially careful to make an independent list of goals when you buy property. Decide that you absolutely positively *won't* buy *anything* until you've seen at least a dozen houses. And write this down a hundred times so you won't be manipulated by a broker pushing the latest fad: *People do well when they buy VALUE, not when they buy what's fashionable.*

Once you've listed and planned how to cope with your real weaknesses, you'll be left with only irrational fears. You can recognize that your fears are irrational and take steps to cope with them.

One alternative is to seek a partnership with a friend you consider a savvy financial person. If that's not practical, most fearful people should try to use a housing purchase as an experiment in business. Start looking for a home to buy (or, if you already own a home, for a home that will be better than your present home after you've fixed it up). Buy carefully, following the advice I gave in chapters 3 and 5.

After you've owned the home for a year or so, go to a real estate agent and evaluate how much equity you now possess. Probably you'll be surprised to discover that you've already made a nice profit (though sometimes it can take two or three years for the profit to show up).

If you don't find that you've made a profit, you'll probably realize that you didn't handle the purchase as you should have. (The most common mistake is avoiding the "risk" of buying a property with things wrong with it.) Ask the broker the value of some properties that you passed up because they were too dirty. You'll probably come away believing that you *could* have made money and understanding how you *should* have done it.

"I Don't Want (or Can't Afford) to Be Tied Down"

Many people fear to invest because they fear they'll want to move away from an area.

If you really expect to move far away very soon, then you should think about investing in the town you're moving to, not the place you're leaving. Often people moving into an area have a fresh eye that helps them pick out properties that will rise in value.

If your fear is just a vague sense that "maybe" you'll want to move, however, then start looking for an opportunity to invest now where you are. You can usually make maximum profits buying and selling in a year and a half.

And if you select your property carefully and do such minimal maintenance as painting and cleaning, be confident you can get back at least the money you put in if you need to sell the property on a month's notice.

You should never get yourself into a position where you need to get your money out that quickly. A forced sale can cost you all the profit you should have made for yourself. But if you buy carefully, you *can* find properties that will be worth significantly more as soon as you've painted them. If you're tempted to avoid investing, remember that the risk that you may have to sell quickly is largely a risk that you may lose your profit, not a risk that you'll take a significant loss.

"I'm Not Motivated by Money"

Embarrassment is one of the biggest factors keeping people from managing their money intelligently. We all know at least one or two boring people who brag about how much money they've made on investments. They're obnoxious, and we don't want to be like them. An investment that does nothing but make money really is crass compared to more intellectual pursuits — or compared to an investment that creates something worthwhile and new.

I have no interest in people who spend all their time at cocktail parties talking about how much their condo has risen in value. Most of the people I've quoted in this book don't easily talk about their economic strategies. Their assets have given them freedom to pursue other activities. They don't brag. Moreover, sometimes people who have created something really worthwhile have lived with it so intimately that they can't easily talk about it. (One reason why so few people know how to create wealth usefully is that those who do it well rarely talk about it.)

But there's no reason to subsist through life on a salary just because *some* people who make money talk about it crassly and those who are truly admirable may not talk about it at all. You can build independence for yourself and do more for others at the same time by managing your assets creatively. When you buy a property and improve it, or when you create or finance a business, you make money because you're doing something useful. And when you have built some resources for yourself, your ability to spend your life in other worthwhile activities increases enormously.

People who are embarrassed thinking about money are often those who most need to think about how they'll get where they want to be in five or ten years. If you plan how to build some wealth, you'll be able to live the kind of life you think is right.

Starting Now

To put the strategies in this book into practice, by now you should have

- made some notes on life goals,
- produced a simple balance sheet,
- worked out a bit of strategy for your life, and
- begun planning your first (or your next) investment.

Now you need to nurture that investment plan to fruition. Plan to refer to this book (and perhaps some of the other books listed in Appendix B) at least once a month for the next few years. For the next few months, ask yourself regularly how much you've done to further your plans. If you haven't made significant progress by the end of three or four months, you probably need to write out a timetable for your investment planning and make sure you stick reasonably close to it. You'll find you really *can* get ahead — but you may need to discipline yourself at first.

If after eighteen months to two years you can honestly say you've managed your resources as I suggest and you haven't made dramatic progress toward your goals, you have my permission to throw this book into the trash.

A Little Bit of Wealth

You can and should build a little bit of wealth. Think about what you want to do in life and then simply follow the Smart-Money

Spiral: Find a piece of property that's fallen on hard times and available at a good price. Buy it. Improve it. Then either sell it or borrow against it. Buy more property that needs improving. Or find something that people either need or want or can be made to want. Set up a business that gives it to them. Or invest in someone else's business that will do it.

There's really no trick to managing resources. When you've become prosperous, don't be boorish. But do tell your friends about the book that helped you get started.

A Sample Partnership Agreement

If you form a partnership or other business arrangement with friends, you'll want to write your own partnership agreement. But study this sample, which is based on an agreement between two people planning to buy and renovate buildings together. It should give you ideas about how to proceed.

Note that this agreement makes provision for more than two partners although only two partners are participating initially. This is often worthwhile because it means that the original partnership agreement can continue in force with little or no amendment if you later add partners.

After you've written an agreement, it's a good idea to show it to a lawyer, who may suggest items that should be included, left out, or changed.

Partnership Agreement

1. Introduction
This is a partnership agreement made on (*date*) between A.B.C. of (*address*) and D.E.F. of (*address*). These two individuals agree to form, and hereby do form, a partnership. (*Your attorney may recommend that you name the state law that will apply to the partnership here.*)

2. Name
The name of the partnership shall be (*whatever you want to call your business*).

3. Purpose

The businesses to be carried on by the partnership are buying, improving, operating, and selling real estate, and whatever other businesses the partners may decide to embark on.

4. Place of Business

The principal place of business of the partnership shall be at (*wherever it will be*), and business may also be conducted at such other places as may be mutually agreed upon. (*If you intend to split duties among partners and different duties may be carried out at different homes, you may want to indicate that each person's home will be one of the "places of business."*)

5. Duration

The partnership shall commence on the date of signing of this agreement and continue until it is dissolved by mutual agreement of the parties.

6. Capital Contribution

The initial capital of the partnership is to be $———. Each partner is to contribute the following amounts:

A.B.C.	$——
D.E.F.	$——

The contributions of the partners must be made on or before (*some appropriate date*) or this agreement will be void.

7. Sharing Profits and Losses

Each of the partners shall share in the profits and losses of the business on the following basis:

A.B.C.	——%
D.E.F.	——%

8. Management and Authority

All partners will have rights in the management of the partnership in direct proportion to their capital contributions. In case of disagreement among the partners, decisions shall be made by majority vote.

9. Division of Responsibility

(*Here it's a good idea to list how you intend to divide responsibility within the business.*)

All permits and licenses will be held in the name of the business, and will not be held individually by any partner.

This division of responsibility may be altered at any time by mutual agreement of the partners.

10. Books of Account

Books of account of the transactions of the partnership shall be the primary responsibility of——and shall be kept at——.

Any partner may inspect them at any time. Each partner will cause to be entered on the books an accurate account of all his dealings, receipts, and expenditures on behalf of the partnership.

11. Fiscal Year

The fiscal year of the partnership shall begin on the first day of January of each year.

12. Annual Accounting and Inventory

In December of each year, a complete inventory of the property and other assets of the partnership will be taken, and a complete statement of the condition of the partnership will be made. The profits and losses of the preceding year shall then be divided and paid or contributed according to the formula in the section titled "Sharing of Profits and Losses," above.

13. Restrictions on Powers of Partners

Any one partner can spend or obligate the partnership to spend up to $500 in the name of the partnership in any one instance without obtaining consent of the other partner(s).

None of the partners, however, may without the consent of the other partner(s) spend or obligate the partnership to spend more than $500 without the consent of the other partner(s) or without following such procedures as the partner(s) may establish.

None of the partners may, without the consent of the other partner(s), allow the partnership to become obligated as surety for any other person, or lend, spend, give, or take for personal use any part of the partnership property.

14. The Addition of New Partners

The addition of any new partner or partners to this partnership may be done only by unanimous agreement of the partners on such terms and conditions as they agree on.

15. Retirement

Any partner may retire from the partnership at the expiration of any fiscal year on giving the other partner(s) 90 days' written notice of his intention to do so.

16. Procedures in the Event of a Partner's Withdrawal

In the event of the retirement, death, or withdrawal for any other reason of any partner, the business may be dissolved, as indicated in the section titled "Dissolution," below. However, the remaining partner(s) may, if he so desires, continue the business. In the event the remaining partner(s) so chooses, he shall have the right to purchase the interest of the other partner in the business's assets and goodwill by paying to that partner or legal representatives of that partner the value of such interest, calculated as set forth below:

(1) Appraisers The partner(s) desiring to continue the business shall appoint one appraiser and the withdrawing partner or the legal representative of a deceased or incapacitated partner shall appoint one individual as an appraiser. These appraisers shall determine the value of the assets of the partnership. The partners desiring to continue the business will pay to the withdrawing partner or legal representatives of the withdrawing partner an amount equal to the withdrawing partner's share in the determined value of the assets. The withdrawing partner or the legal representative of the withdrawing partner shall execute such documents as may be necessary to convey such partner's interest in the partnership to the other partners.

(2) Additional Appraiser in the Event of Disagreement In the event the appraisers are unable to agree on the value of the assets of the partnership, they shall select one additional appraiser whose appointment will be binding on all parties. In the event that the two appraisers first appointed are unable to agree on a third appraiser, the third appraiser shall be appointed by the presiding judge of (*whatever local court is appropriate*).

(3) Withdrawal of a Chosen Appraiser In the event any appraiser becomes unable or unwillng for any reason to serve, a substitute

shall be appointed by the person or persons originally selecting him.

In the event of the withdrawal of a partner and the continuation of the business, the partner(s) continuing the business shall assume all existing obligations of the partnership and shall indemnify the withdrawing partner or the legal representative of the partner against any liability thereon. The partner(s) continuing the business may continue to use the partnership name.

17. Sale or Transfer of Interest in This Partnership

In the event that a partner wants to sell his interest in the partnership, the remaining partner(s) will have a right of first refusal to purchase it.

In the event that a partner's interest is transferred to a third party, whether by sale, assignment, or other means, the business can continue. It is agreed and understood that any new associate or associates will receive the profits (or assume the losses) to which the transferring partner would have been entitled.

However, unless the other partner(s) agrees in writing prior to the transfer, the new associate or associates shall not be deemed partners. The new associate or associates shall not have the legal rights of a partner nor any of the management rights of the original partner except that they may request a financial accounting on a regular basis.

18. Expulsion from the Partnership

A partner shall cease to be a partner and shall be deemed a seller of his share of the partnership's assets if any of the following occurs:

- The partner obtains or becomes subject to an order for relief under the Bankruptcy code;
- The partner makes an assignment for the benefit of creditors;
- The partner consents to or suffers the appointment of a receiver or trustee to any substantial part of his assets; or
- The partner consents to or suffers an attachment or execution on any substantial part of his assets.

The partner shall be paid a price for his share in the partnership determined in the manner described in the section titled "Procedures in the Event of a Partner's Withdrawal," above.

If a partner is expelled for any of these reasons, the partnership shall not be dissolved, but shall continue to function without interruption.

19. Dissolution
In the event that all the partners agree to dissolve the partnership, the business shall be wound up, the debts paid, and the surplus divided among the partners in accordance with their respective interests therein.

20. Amendments
This agreement, except with respect to vested rights of partners, may be amended at any time by a majority vote as measured by the interest in the sharing of profits and losses.

Supplementary Agreement Between Spouses

If one or more of the partners is married to someone who is not part of the partnership, it may be wise to ask the spouse or spouses to sign an agreement like the following to indicate that they have agreed to the terms of the partnership agreement:

We certify that:

We are the spouses of the persons who signed the foregoing Partnership Agreement dated (*date*) to form (*name of business*).

We have read and approve the provisions of that Partnership Agreement relating to the purchase, sale, or other disposition of the interest of a deceased, withdrawing, or expelled partner.

We agree to accept and be bound by those provisions and any other applicable provisions of the partnership agreement in lieu of any other interests any of us may have in that partnership, whether the interest may be community property interest or otherwise.

Selected Reading List

I. Stocks and Securities

The Intelligent Investor by Benjamin Graham.
A classic. The best analysis on the stock market available.
(Harper & Row: revised edition, 1973)

A Random Walk Down Wall Street by Burton G. Malkiel
This is a personal, first-person guide to stock investment. Malkiel uses simple language to explain different risk-taking outlooks, fundamental and technical analysis, and other basics.
(W. W. Norton & Company: revised fourth edition, 1984)

The Dance of the Money Bees: A Professional Speaks Frankly on Investing by John Train
This book is structured so that sections are self-explanatory to readers skimming the book. Train, a professional investment counselor, emphasizes the need to preserve capital. A glossary is provided.
(Harper & Row: 1974)

The Aggressive Conservative Investor by Martin J. Whitman and Martin Shubik
Two business professors write about stocks and securities. The authors expound on the "financial-integrity approach" to investing, explain "modern capital theory" in terms of individual portfolios, and give a lesson on financial accounting and accounting principles. This book differs from the dozens of "Get Rich in the Stock Market" guides in that it strives to be academic as well as practical,

providing valuable information about how corporate decisions are made.
(Random House: 1979)

II. Real Estate

Barron's Real Estate Handbook by Jack C. Harris and Jack P. Friedman

Written with the professional real estate investor in mind, this book is helpful to anyone considering the field. It is essentially an encyclopedia: everything having to do with real estate investment is listed alphabetically, often with illustrations. The last 260 pages consist of tables: mortgage payments, loan progress, mortgage value, depreciation, etc.
(Barron's Educational Series: 1984)

Nothing Down by Robert G. Allen

A useful guide to getting started in aggressive real estate investing.
(Simon & Schuster: 1984)

The Reader's Digest Complete Do-It-Yourself Manual

How to choose and use hand tools. How to work with wood, concrete, etc. Available by direct mail and telephone. Call 1-800-262-2627 in New York State and 1-800-431-1246 elsewhere.
(Reader's Digest Association)

Real Estate Investment by John P. Wiedemer

This is a textbook covering all the fundamental, and many of the advanced, aspects of real estate investing. Subjects covered include analysis, taxation, land use, business organization, finance, and different types of real estate and forms of investment. It is a dense book, dry in tone and filled with graphs and tables. The ten page glossary is valuable.
(Reston Publishing Company: 1979)

The Complete Real Estate Advisor by Daniel J. deBenedictis

Billing itself as "the layman's guide to today's real estate market," this book covers just about every aspect of the field of concern to the nonprofessional. Chapters are devoted to buying real estate for a family, advice to the seller, real estate laws, practical ways of making money on real estate, mortgage financing, and how a broker makes money. This basic, comprehensive guide provides sample letters and contracts and warns of the many pitfalls and tricks that the beginning real estate investor must watch for.

(Simon & Schuster: 1977, 1983)

III. Starting a Business

New Business Ventures and the Entrepreneur by Howard H. Stevenson, Michael J. Roberts, and H. Irving Grousbeck

A "how-to" book by faculty members of the Harvard Business School. The case studies are very good.

(Richard D. Irwin: 1985)

Raising Venture Capital (First Book of the Entrepreneur's Guidebook Series) by Deloitte Haskins & Sells

This is a flashy, high-tech pamphlet that tells how to start a business, from naming the enterprise to negotiating with venture capitalists. Utilizing lists of "factoids," it doesn't pretend to provide in-depth analysis. It does, however, provide sample business plans, balance sheets, and financial forecasts.

(DHS High Technology Industry Group: 1982)

How to Prepare and Present a Business Plan by Joseph Mancuso

A straightforward book aimed at the beginner, it contains all the necessary information about form and legality. Mancuso, who gives seminars on this topic, goes to lengths to explain what venture capitalists, consultants, bankers, and lawyers look for when reading a business plan. Entrepreneurial examples are given in the text. Case studies, tables, and sample business plans are provided in appendixes.

(Prentice Hall: 1983)

Planning and Financing Your Own Business by John McKiernan

"What," asks this book, "triggers an otherwise normal human being to forgo the safety, security and sanity of a regular job to attempt to start his or her own business?"

The first five chapters give adequate treatment to the mechanisms of venture capital: market research, planning, raising capital, the entrepreneur, etc. The last two-thirds of the book list sources of venture capital: corporations, partnerships, and individuals, with addresses and telephone numbers, who can be approached for venture capital deals.

(Technology Management Inc.: 1978; distributed by Management Associates, P.O. Box 230, Chestnut Hill, Mass. 02167)

Handbook of Business Finance & Capital Sources by Dileep Rao, Ph.D.

The first 130 pages are a technical explanation of capital acquisition. The rest of the book is an exhaustive listing of capital sources, listed under such headings as Commercial Finance, Leasing Companies, Mutual Savings Banks, and State Institutions and Programs. Information given about each source includes the range in amount of loans given, industries the lender prefers to invest in, and preferred business characteristics of lendees. Every entrepreneur should acquaint him- or herself with this reference book.

(Interfinance Corporation: 1982)

IV. Taxation

Your Federal Income Tax by the Internal Revenue Service

A free booklet explaining the tax system. Don't expect to find any unique ways to save money on taxes in the booklet.

Miller's Personal Income Tax Guide: 1984 by Martin A. Miller

A practical guide with helpful worksheets.

(Harcourt Brace Jovanavich: 1983)

How to Do Business with the I.R.S. by Randy Bruce Blaustein, Esq.

A lawyer and former Internal Revenue Service agent provides information on how to survive a tax audit, encompassing everything a person should do from the moment notice is received. While the book's scope is fairly narrow, it is valuable in gaining an understanding of the IRS — sections tell about the agency's internal organization, of techniques it uses to develop a criminal case, and simply how to put off paying taxes and avoid paying penalties.

(Prentice Hall: 1984)

Taxation and Business Planning by Houstin Shockey, Henry Sweeney, and Gerald Brady

The self-proclaimed purpose of this book is to "describe the general tax effects of the main ways of organizing, conducting, and liquidating American businesses. . . ." In dry prose, it explains business forms, election of taxable status, investment trusts, use of multiple business forms, family partnerships, compensation of employee shareholders, constructive ownership of stock, and much more.

(Prentice Hall: 1963)

V. Negotiating

Getting to Yes by Roger Fisher and William Ury

A best-seller available in most bookstores, *Getting to Yes* contains the authors' method of settling disagreements with neither side giving in. As useful for marital disputes as for business deals (although aimed at business people), this book uses simple language and gives more weight to concepts like "trust" and "emotion" than to complicated theory and graphs. An enjoyable, short read.

(Penguin: 1983)

VI. IRA's

The IRA Book by Robert Krufhoff et al.

In simple language, this long pamphlet explains how IRA's may have a place in the layman's overall investment package. The chapters are short — divided under innumerable subheadings — and try to answer the beginner's questions. Graphically, *The IRA Book* is a pleasure. Sections are broken up by illustrations and easily accessible graphs and tables before they can get boring. Aside from its information on IRAs, this book provides valuable assistance in overall retirement planning, and comes with worksheets that compare the various forms of savings and investments.

(Center for the Study of Services: 1984)

Your Complete Guide to IRA's & Keoghs by Jack Egan

A comprehensive guide to the subject, explained in an easy-to-understand manner. Contains more than you need to know about the programs.

(Harper & Row: 1982)